ALL-IN-ONE DUTCH OVEN COOKBOOK FOR TWO

all-in-one
DUTCH OVEN
COOKBOOK for two

One-Pot Meals
You'll Both Love

JANET A. ZIMMERMAN

ROCKRIDGE
PRESS

As always, to Dave.

And to the late Steven Shaw, my dear friend who gave me my first food writing assignment and who shared my obsession with miniature Dutch ovens.

Contents

Introduction
The Joy of Going Dutch

When I got my first bonus at my first real job, I went shopping and splurged on Le Creuset cookware. Along with a couple of skillets and a small saucepan, I picked up two Dutch ovens—one small and one large. Although I'd been cooking for years by then, it was by far the best cookware I'd ever owned or worked with in the kitchen. It made cooking a joy instead of a chore.

The Dutch ovens saw heavy use. I realized that, with them, I could finally make some of my favorite recipes from my childhood. I'd never before had anything large or sturdy enough to cook Mom's chicken and dumplings or Dad's navy bean soup. Since it was by far my largest pot, I used the 4.5-quart Dutch oven for all kinds of things, from boiling pasta to deep-frying to roasting chickens, but that little one was equally useful. It became my baking dish, because it was such a good size for small batches. As my cooking skills increased, I outgrew most of my older pieces of cookware, but I never outgrew my Dutch ovens.

Little did I know it back then, but I would eventually make a living from cooking, not as a chef or even a line cook, but as a cooking instructor, recipe developer, and food writer. One of my specialties is creating recipes for two, so I spend much of my time reducing and adapting larger recipes to make them work for two servings. And since my partner and I cook mostly for just the two of us, developing great recipes that feed two people is as personal as it is professional.

Over the years, my Dutch ovens continued to be mainstays in our kitchen. They're especially useful in making "one-pot" meals, which are great for when we don't feel like making separate courses or extra side dishes, but they're also the go-to for searing meat, deep-frying, and baking.

And that's the beauty of a Dutch oven. Its versatility and durability make it one of the most-used—and most useful—pieces of cookware. I hope that you'll grow to love your Dutch oven as much as we love ours.

ONE POT, COUNTLESS MEALS

Today's home cooks are exposed to what can seem like an endless array of cookware—different materials, different designs, and different pieces—on cooking shows, shopping networks, or online. Some buy a lot of cookware, and some don't, but one thing that experienced cooks agree on is the importance of having a few really dependable, versatile tools. The Dutch oven is one such tool; in fact, some would claim it's the only pot you need. Beyond braising meats and slow-cooking stews, it produces an amazing variety of meals from Cajun gumbo and Chinese stir-fries to Indian lentils and Thai curries. What you might not realize, though, is that a Dutch oven is just as useful for serving two as it can be when serving a crowd.

A Traditional Staple for a Modern Kitchen

Dutch ovens have been around for so long in so many kitchens that they might seem a bit old-fashioned for today's cook. I remember my mother, aunts, and grandmother cooking with them, making big batches of turkey soup the day after Thanksgiving. But for many of us, there is a desire to simplify our cooking and our kitchens. Perhaps as a backlash to the multitude of products available, the modern kitchen is the minimal kitchen, where less is more. The Dutch oven then becomes invaluable to today's cook. When you can use one pot to make an entire meal, dinner doesn't seem like such an onerous task. This is true whether you're cooking for a family or just for two.

That's where this book comes in. You'll find recipes for just the two of you, using (in most cases) one pot and a few tools, and creating a minimum of mess. The vast majority—everything but breads and desserts—are all-in-one meals, so side dishes are unnecessary, which makes both cooking and cleaning up easier.

What Is a Dutch Oven?

In the broadest terms, a Dutch oven is a heavy pot with short handles and a lid, which can be used both on the stove top and in the oven.

Although they can be made from different materials, the most popular Dutch ovens are made from cast iron—that is, iron cast in dry sand molds. Iron is an extremely dense metal, slow to heat up, but also slow to let heat go. This quality helps reduce the temperature fluctuations when compared to other cookware.

The first Dutch ovens were uncoated pots with tight-fitting lids and legs, which kept the body of the pot out of the fire. You can still purchase such pots; they are often called camp ovens.

While uncoated cast iron ovens and camp ovens require seasoning before use (see page 12) and must be handwashed, more modern enameled cast iron Dutch ovens are rustproof, dishwasher safe, and require less maintenance. By nature, their smooth surface is stick-resistant and they can be used right away, with no seasoning needed.

While the method for casting metal in dry sand molds probably originated in the Netherlands (hence the name "Dutch oven"), cast iron Dutch ovens came to America by way of Britain, where they were being manufactured by the early 1700s. Their durability and versatility made them a valuable tool both in colonial kitchens and outdoors in army, trappers', or explorers' camps. Heavy iron pots were ideal for campfires, especially with the legs that kept the pots up out of the fire and handles that could hang them up over the fire for long-cooked stews. As American settlers moved West, their Dutch ovens went with them.

But these pots were also indispensable in kitchens, from farmhouses to settlers' cabins to city dwellings. Iron's capacity for retaining heat meant that less fuel was necessary to cook food, and their durability meant that they'd last for generations. Their versatility meant that they could be used for tasks from braising stews to baking cakes; in kitchens with few cooking vessels, this was essential to getting dinner on the table. Even as more cookware in new shapes and new materials became available to American cooks, the reliable, durable Dutch oven always kept its place on the stove.

How the Dutch Oven Works

A Dutch oven can produce some relatively quick weeknight meals, but it truly excels in recipes that call for long, slow cooking, like soups, stews, and braises. The density of cast iron keeps the temperature of these dishes constant with little or no attention, whether you're cooking on the stove top or in the oven. While it may take an hour or more for a dish to cook in a Dutch oven, after the initial prep work you can ignore it for long periods of time and still end up with fantastically flavored meals. With some care it cleans up easily (see page 207), and since many meals can be cooked start to finish in one Dutch oven, you're not left with a sink full of dishes after dinner.

THE SKINNY ON SEASONING AND MAINTENANCE

If your Dutch oven is not enameled, you'll need to season it. Think of seasoning cast iron as an on-going process, not a one-time event. The purpose of seasoning is to create a smoother cooking surface. Once it's seasoned, you can treat your cast iron Dutch oven as if it were a piece of nonstick cookware or enameled cast iron, using the same utensils.

Even if your cast iron Dutch oven came "preseasoned," here's what you need to do before using:

> Heat your oven to 450°F.

> Using hot, soapy water, wash and thoroughly dry the pot.

> With a paper towel dipped in oil (canola, vegetable, or corn will do), rub your pan all over, including the handle and bottom.

> Put the pan in the oven for 30 minutes. It will smoke; that's okay. Take it out and let it cool.

> Repeat steps 3 and 4 a few times, until the pan turns deep black.

To care for it, wash the Dutch oven promptly with dishwashing liquid and the scrubby side of a sponge if necessary (neither will damage a well-seasoned pot) and dry it immediately. Apply oil to it after washing and drying it, and use it a lot. It will improve with age.

The Benefits of an Indoor Dutch Oven

If you already cook with a Dutch oven, you know how handy this durable workhorse can be. If you need some persuading, here are just a few of the benefits:

SPACE SAVER In a small kitchen without much storage, a Dutch oven can fill in for a number of other pieces of cookware (see "Yes, Your Dutch Oven Can Cook It," page 19). In the words of Food Network's Alton Brown, they're multitaskers, which is great if you're a newlywed in a small apartment or an empty nester looking to downsize your kitchen. As a bonus, the Dutch oven is great for making one-pot meals, allowing you to cook a balanced dinner in less time with less fuss.

EASY CLEAN UP Dutch ovens can go from the stove to the oven to the table, which means fewer dishes to clean. And enameled Dutch ovens look beautiful on the table.

UNATTENDED COOKING The dishes at which a Dutch oven excels—soups, stews, and braises—can cook relatively unattended, which means you can spend less time at the stove and still turn out delicious meals.

VERSATILITY A wide variety of brands and sizes of Dutch ovens are available. While they aren't cheap, they range in affordability. Whether you have $75 or $375 to plunk down on a Dutch oven, you'll be able to find a good one for your budget.

FLEXIBILITY Many Dutch oven recipes are prepared in steps, which can be done at one time, or broken up and finished at different times. This flexibility can really make a difference if you and your partner have different schedules; one can start a recipe on Sunday afternoon and the other can finish it Monday in time for dinner.

Which Size Dutch Oven Is Best?

Dutch ovens come in sizes from 1 cup (Le Creuset sells tiny individual pots made just like their big brothers) up to a 15-quart "goose pot" that is not only large enough to cook a goose, but also to bathe a small child. Realistically, though, most cooks consider sizes between 2 quarts and 7 quarts, with the 5- to 6-quart sizes being the most popular.

When you're cooking for two, it might seem that you want to stick with the smaller sizes (2 quarts to 3 quarts), and in some cases these smaller sizes are ideal. However, for many recipes, a larger size is better—for instance, you can't cook pasta for two in a 2-quart pot. I tested the recipes in the book using a 5-quart and a 6-quart Dutch oven, but with very few exceptions, the dishes will turn out fine in any size pot from 3.5 quarts up to 6 quarts.

Considerations for Different Sizes

Depending on which size Dutch oven you use, you will need to make a few adjustments and keep in mind some size-related considerations. Here's what you need to know:

BUTTER OR OIL The amount of oil or butter it takes to coat the bottom of the pot (or fill it up for deep- or shallow-frying) will vary depending on its size. That's why you'll find a range of amounts of those ingredients.

TOPPINGS Likewise, the amounts of any toppings (the panko topping for the Macaroni and Cheese on page 84, for instance) will also depend on the pan size. The larger the pot, the more topping will be required to cover the entire dish.

LIQUID Finally, the amount of braising liquid necessary will be greater for a large pot than a small pot, and you should make adjustments to get the proper liquid level.

RESULTS While the recipes will work with various sizes of Dutch oven, you'll notice some different results in some of the finished dishes. For instance, in the Baked Eggs Florentine recipe (see page 22), if you have a 5-quart pot, the spinach base will form a thin layer—not really deep enough to form the indentations for the eggs. A smaller pot will yield a deeper layer, so you'll be able to form nests for the eggs. On the other hand, if the pot is too small, you'll only be able to fit two eggs, rather than four.

If you're serious about making small batch desserts (two large or four small servings) you may want to consider a 2-quart oven. That's because in baking, pan size is crucial. For more information, see the individual dessert recipes in Chapter 8.

DUTCH OVENS MOSTLY CREATED EQUAL

Dutch ovens come in a wide variety of colors, sizes, and shapes, and they're also available at various price levels.

Generally speaking, plain cast iron (the best-known brand is Lodge) is less expensive than enameled cast iron. The best-known enameled Dutch oven in the US is made by the French company Le Creuset, with Staub, another French maker, a close second. While both of these brands have a colored, high-gloss enamel exterior, Staub's interior is a black matte enamel; Le Creuset's is a light-colored high-gloss enamel. Does that matter? In my experience, not a lot. The dark interior of Staub seems to be slightly better for searing meat, but it's easier to see the layer of browned bits in the Le Creuset pot, and therefore easier to make sure you get it all dissolved. Both are easy to clean, and both are dishwasher safe.

In the last 10 years or so, numerous other brands have appeared, often licensed by such food personalities as Mario Batali and Martha Stewart. Lodge has also come out with an enameled line of pots, which tend to be less expensive than Staub and Le Creuset. They are also often lighter in weight than either of those two brands, but the main

difference seems to be in the enamel coating, which in my personal experience is not as durable as what you'll find in a French oven.

Chances are, if you're reading this book, you already have a Dutch oven. If you don't, or if you're in the market for a second one, find the heaviest one you can at the price you can afford. If you can find a Le Creuset or Staub on sale or at an outlet or second-hand store, consider those brands, even if it means you end up with a color that might not necessarily have been your first choice. That said, the less expensive brands make fine Dutch ovens, if slightly less durable, that will serve you well.

The Seven Commandments of Dutch Oven Use

The Dutch oven might be thought of as the original slow cooker. And fortunately it doesn't need a manual for use; it's pretty intuitive. But if you want to get the most out of meals cooked with a Dutch oven, here's a handy overview of my best tips.

1. *No sharp utensils.* This isn't a safety recommendation for you but rather for the Dutch oven. A sharp-edged metal spatula, or even a fork's tines, can damage the enamel or seasoning on your pot.

2. *Use long, silicone-tipped tongs.* These tongs are a must-have for turning foods as you brown them. The deep sides of a Dutch oven keep splattering to a minimum, but they also make it easy to burn your arms if your utensils don't reach easily into the pot.

3. *Keep oven mitts close by.* Always assume that the pot handles and knob on the lid are hot. Whether you use it on the stove or in the oven, there's no such thing as a stay-cool handle on a Dutch oven.

4. *Two hands at all times.* Don't try to move your Dutch oven with one hand. While you can use one hand to lift a lighter pan with a long handle, you can't do that with a heavy, short-handled pot. And trust me, it isn't easy to cook with a sprained wrist.

5. *Deglaze your Dutch oven.* Leaving browned bits of food stuck on the bottom of a Dutch oven leads to burned food later on. Deglaze the pot by adding liquid to dissolve it. If you don't already have one, buy a wok spatula or similar utensil in wood or silicone and use for deglazing. A wok spatula is angled on the bottom, with one curved side and one straight side, for getting into corners.

6. *Don't put a hot Dutch oven into cold water.* Thermal shock can damage the enamel, and even plain cast iron can split if subjected to extreme temperature changes. Let your Dutch oven come to room temperature before submerging it in cold or cool water.

7. *Invest in a deep-fry thermometer.* You'll need it if you plan to deep-fry in your Dutch oven. Overheating oil can be dangerous for you and bad for your pot, and oil that's not hot enough will produce greasy food.

Shopping for Two

When you're shopping for two, a regular grocery store can seem like a big box store—everything comes in larger sizes than you need. But there are ways to navigate and avoid waste when shopping.

> Shop in a market with actual meat and seafood counters, where you can buy individual steaks or fillets rather than just packages.

> Get to know the staff at your local grocery store. Don't see a half-pound package of ground beef when that's all you need? Ask the person working the meat counter, and it's likely they can accommodate you. If all you need is half a cabbage or butternut squash, it's possible that whoever is stocking produce will cut it if you ask politely.

> The bulk section is your best friend. Seek out a market that sells ingredients such as nuts, grains, and spices in bulk. By purchasing from those bins, you will only buy the amount you need, and you'll likely save money, since bulk items are often cheaper than packaged goods.

> Don't dismiss the frozen foods section. Many fruits and vegetables freeze quite well, and packages of frozen produce will last much longer than their fresh counterparts. Bags of individually frozen raw shrimp or fish fillets can be a boon when you're cooking for two.

This Book's Recipes

All the recipes in this book are written for two people. Since it's impossible to gauge the appetite of all readers, I've created most of the recipes to produce two generous portions, or two moderate portions with some leftovers (for lunch or a light dinner). Some of the dessert and bread recipes will make two large or four small servings. However, to accommodate cooks who don't have a small Dutch oven but still want to bake desserts, some recipes are written with ingredient amounts both for a large batch (6 to 8 servings, in a 5- to 6-quart pot) and a small batch (3 to 4 servings, in a 2- to 3-quart pot).

With very few exceptions, all of the recipes can be made entirely in one Dutch oven. However, in some cases that means using the Dutch oven sequentially for different steps—such as cooking pasta first, then making a sauce, then combining the two. With those recipes, you can save time by doing one or more of the tasks in a different pot. To go with our example, pasta can cook in your Dutch oven while you make the sauce in a sauce pan. Of course, in that case you'll have an extra pan to wash; that decision is up to you.

Each recipe specifies two times: Active Time and Total Time. Active Time includes preparing foods (chopping, mincing, peeling, etc.) as well as hands-on cooking tasks. Total Time is the Active Time plus any unattended cooking or resting time. I assumed average knife skills when calculating the active times; your actual time may vary.

I used a 5-quart Staub and a 5.5-quart Le Creuset Dutch oven to test the recipes. For tips on using other sizes, see "Which Size Dutch Oven Is Best?" on page 13. Any other notes on pot size will appear in the appropriate recipes.

The recipes in this book, with very few exceptions, were developed using Diamond Crystal brand kosher salt. If you use fine salt in the recipes in this book that call for kosher salt, use half as much.

Finally, many of the recipes include tips—ways to make prep go faster, substitutions for hard-to-find ingredients, beverage pairing suggestions, directions for doubling and freezing, and more. Enjoy!

It's common knowledge that Dutch ovens are fabulous at slow cooking soups and pot roast, but if you're not familiar with them, you might not know everything else they can do.

> You can bake bread in your Dutch oven (No-Knead Bread, page 182, or Olive Herb Bread, page 184)

> You can cook custards and cheesecakes in a Dutch oven water bath (Creamy Lemon Cheesecakes, page 200, or Coffee Pots de Crème, page 202)

> A Dutch oven makes an excellent deep fryer (Baja Fish Tacos with Avocado Cream, page 96)

> If you flip it over, a Dutch oven can double as a baking stone for small pizzas or galettes (Mixed Fruit Galette, page 198)

> Your Dutch oven can stand in for a wok when cooking stir-fry dishes (Chinese Pepper Steak Stir-Fry, page 160, or Stir-Fried Pork with Tangerines and Bok Choy, page 150)

EGGS & THINGS

chapter
two

Baked Eggs Florentine

ACTIVE TIME
30 MINUTES

TOTAL TIME
40 MINUTES

Serves 2

Bacon and spinach go together deliciously, and the addition of heavy cream, eggs, and cheese make this a downright decadent dish. If you've never cooked raw spinach before, one pound might seem like way too much for two people but, as it cooks, it significantly reduces in volume. If you buy spinach by the 9-ounce bag, simply use two bags.

2 to 3 slices bacon, diced

1 pound baby spinach

¾ cup heavy cream

2 garlic cloves, minced

Kosher salt

⅛ teaspoon freshly ground white or black pepper

2 teaspoons butter, melted

3 tablespoons grated Parmigiano-Reggiano or similar cheese

½ cup panko bread crumbs

2 to 4 large eggs

1. Preheat the oven to 375°F.

2. Place the Dutch oven over medium heat. Add the bacon and stir to separate the pieces. Cook, stirring occasionally, until the bacon is crisp and has rendered most of its fat. Remove the bacon pieces to a paper towel–lined plate, leaving the fat in the pot.

3. By the handful, add the spinach to the pot, stirring to wilt it, and adding more as soon as there is room. It should take 4 batches or so. Remove the spinach to a colander and press with the back of a large spoon to drain off as much liquid as possible.

4. Pour the cream into the Dutch oven and add the garlic. Cook for 3 minutes, or until the cream has reduced by about one-third. Season with salt, stir in the pepper, and add the spinach back to the pot. Stir to distribute the cream and bring the mixture to a simmer.

5. While the mixture heats, in a small bowl, stir together the butter, cheese, and panko.

6. Sprinkle the reserved bacon over the surface of the spinach. With the back of the spoon, make an indentation in the spinach mixture for each egg you're using. (Depending on the size of your Dutch oven, the spinach might not be deep enough for this.) Crack the eggs into the indentations and sprinkle the panko mixture over the surface of the eggs, or the entire spinach mixture (if you have enough). Place the pot, uncovered, into the preheated oven. Bake for 8 to 10 minutes, or until the eggs are done to your liking.

7. To serve, spoon some spinach and eggs into two bowls, being careful not to break the eggs.

INGREDIENT TIP You can turn this into a vegetarian dish by substituting cooked mushrooms for the bacon, and olive oil or butter for the bacon fat. Cook the mushrooms according to the method in the Mushroom and Shallot Soup with Chives recipe (page 46).

Shakshuka

ACTIVE TIME
40 MINUTES

TOTAL TIME
40 MINUTES

Serves 2

VEGETARIAN

Once in a while, a dish will become wildly popular, seemingly overnight. Shakshuka (also spelled shakshouka) is one of those dishes. Similar to "eggs in purgatory," this Middle Eastern spicy sauce and egg dish sometimes contains feta cheese. For neater-looking eggs, crack them into a small strainer to drain off the thin whites before adding to the sauce.

2 to 3 tablespoons olive oil

½ small onion, chopped (about ⅓ cup)

½ medium red or green bell pepper, seeded and chopped (about ⅓ cup)

1 small jalapeño pepper, seeded and minced

2 garlic cloves, chopped, divided

Kosher salt

1 (14.5-ounce) can diced tomatoes with their juice

½ teaspoon ground cumin

½ teaspoon ground sweet paprika

¼ teaspoon freshly ground black pepper

⅓ cup crumbled feta cheese

2 to 4 large eggs

1. Place the Dutch oven over medium heat. Add enough oil to coat the bottom of the pot and heat until the oil shimmers. Add the onion, bell pepper, jalapeño, and half the garlic. Season with salt and cook, stirring occasionally, for about 10 minutes, or until the vegetables are soft.

2. Add the tomatoes, cumin, paprika, and black pepper and bring to a simmer. Cook for 10 minutes, stirring occasionally. Add the remaining garlic and cook for another 5 minutes. For a smoother consistency, use the back of a spoon or a potato masher to break up the tomatoes. Taste and adjust the seasoning. Gently stir in the feta cheese.

3. With the sauce still at a simmer, gently crack the eggs onto the surface. Cover the Dutch oven and cook for about 3 minutes, then remove the cover. Baste the tops of the eggs with some of the sauce and cook until the eggs are done to your liking, 3 to 5 more minutes, continuing to baste once or twice more.

Corned Beef Hash with Eggs

ACTIVE TIME
30 MINUTES

TOTAL TIME
40 MINUTES

Serves 2

When it comes to hash, there seem to be two schools: those who prefer separate pieces of potato and meat, and those who like it more like a coarse mash. This method splits the difference. The potatoes and meat are separate cubes, but the sauce makes a more cohesive dish. While hash and eggs is a classic brunch dish, we often have this for dinner since it's so filling.

2 to 3 tablespoons olive or vegetable oil

1 to 2 small Yukon Gold potatoes, peeled and diced into ¼-inch cubes

1 very small onion, diced (about ½ cup)

Kosher salt

6 ounces (about 2 cups) cooked corned beef, diced into ¼-inch cubes

½ cup chicken or beef stock

1 to 2 tablespoons heavy cream

Freshly ground black pepper

2 to 4 large eggs

1. Preheat the oven to 375°F.

2. Place the Dutch oven over medium heat. Add enough oil to coat the bottom of the pot and heat until the oil shimmers. Add the potatoes in a single layer and cook without stirring for 3 to 4 minutes, or until the bottoms are browned. Use a spatula to flip over the potatoes, then brown for a minute or two and flip again. Try to brown all sides of the potato cubes until they're crispy.

3. If there is still some oil in the pot, add the onion. If the skillet is dry, move the potatoes to the sides of the pan, add another tablespoon of oil in the center, and heat for a minute before adding the onion. Season with salt. Cook, stirring gently, until the onion pieces separate and soften. Try not to break the potato pieces apart. »

4. Add the corned beef and stock and bring the liquid to a simmer, reducing slightly. Stir in the cream and season with salt and black pepper. The hash ingredients should be coated generously with sauce, but not swimming in liquid.

5. If possible, make 2 or 4 indentations in the hash for the eggs. (Depending on the size of your Dutch oven, the hash ingredients might not be deep enough for this.) Crack the eggs into the indentations and place the pot, uncovered, into the preheated oven. Bake for 8 to 10 minutes, or until the eggs are done to your liking.

6. Let cool slightly and serve.

INGREDIENT TIP This recipe is a good way to use up any leftover cooked meat, not just corned beef. Try it with Pot Roast for Two (Really!) (page 158), chicken, or pork.

Root Vegetable Hash and Scrambled Eggs

ACTIVE TIME
20 MINUTES

TOTAL TIME
1 HOUR
20 MINUTES

Serves 2

VEGETARIAN

Perfectly meatless, this nutritious, colorful, and hearty hash-and-egg combo makes breakfast (or breakfast for dinner) worth waiting for. Unlike the Corned Beef Hash with Eggs (page 25), this dish is cooked mostly in the oven, which means it requires very little hands-on work. The only hard thing about it is peeling and dicing the beet and sweet potato, which are both fairly dense. After peeling, cut each vegetable into half lengthwise, and lay it cut-side down, then cut into planks and then dice.

1 very small red beet

1 very small sweet potato

1 small Yukon Gold potato

1 medium carrot

½ medium onion, coarsely chopped

2 to 3 tablespoons olive oil

¼ teaspoon kosher salt, plus more for sprinkling

1 tablespoon butter

3 to 4 large eggs

Freshly ground black pepper

¼ cup grated Parmigiano-Reggiano or similar cheese

1. Preheat the oven to 375°F.

2. Peel the beet, sweet potato, gold potato, and carrot and cut them into pieces about ½ inch on a side.

3. Add the cut vegetables along with the onion to the Dutch oven and drizzle with enough olive oil to coat all the vegetables. Sprinkle with salt and toss to coat. Move the vegetables into an even layer.

4. Place the pot, uncovered, in the hot oven and roast for about 20 minutes. Remove the Dutch oven and stir the vegetables. Return to the oven and roast for another 15 minutes and stir again. Check one of the beet chunks with a small knife or fork to see if it's tender; if not, continue to cook for 10 to 15 minutes. The vegetables should be crisp on the outside but soft inside. »

5. Place the Dutch oven on the stove top over medium-low heat and move the hash to the perimeter of the pot. Add the butter to the center of the Dutch oven.

6. In a small bowl, whisk together the eggs with the remaining ¼ teaspoon of salt while the butter melts. When it's foaming, pour the eggs in and let sit for 30 seconds or so, just until they start to set. Stir the eggs for 1 to 2 minutes. Sprinkle the eggs and vegetables with the pepper and cheese, and either mix the eggs into the vegetables or serve separately.

TECHNIQUE TIP If you prefer, you can skip scrambling the eggs and bake them as in the Corned Beef Hash with Eggs recipe (page 25).

Leek and Red Pepper Frittata

ACTIVE TIME
15 MINUTES

TOTAL TIME
30 MINUTES

Serves 2

VEGETARIAN

Frittatas, the Italian cousins to French omelets, are ordinarily made in a skillet on the stove top, although they are often finished in the oven. A Dutch oven works well for cooking a frittata, with a couple of adjustments. The heat of a Dutch oven will continue to cook the eggs, so take the pot out of the oven when the eggs are barely done, and then cut the frittata and remove the slices quickly so they don't overcook.

3 tablespoons butter

1 small leek, washed, trimmed, and chopped (white and light green parts only)

½ small red bell pepper, seeded and chopped

Kosher salt

5 large eggs

2 tablespoons whole milk

Freshly ground black pepper

½ cup shredded Fontina cheese (or other mild, melting cheese)

1. Preheat the oven to 325°F.

2. Place the Dutch oven over medium heat and add the butter. When it stops foaming, add the leek and bell pepper and season with salt. Cook, stirring, for 3 to 4 minutes, or until the vegetables have softened. Spread them evenly over the bottom of the Dutch oven. Turn the heat to low.

3. In a medium bowl, whisk together the eggs and milk, and season with salt and pepper. Pour into the Dutch oven. Cook over low heat for 2 to 3 minutes, or until the bottom of the eggs set slightly.

4. Move the pot into the oven and cook, uncovered, for 10 to 15 minutes, or until the eggs are beginning to set, with the middle not yet done. Remove from the oven, sprinkle the cheese over the frittata and return to bake for another 5 minutes, or until the cheese is melted and the eggs are just barely set. »

5. Remove from the oven and use a silicone spatula to divide the frittata into 4 to 6 pieces. Remove the slices from the Dutch oven. Let cool slightly. Serve warm or at room temperature.

INGREDIENT TIP Once you get the method and timing down for frittatas, you can add almost any vegetables or cheeses, as well as meat. Just be sure that you cook any vegetables to remove most of their liquid before adding the eggs.

Congee with Eggs and Herbs

ACTIVE TIME
45 MINUTES

TOTAL TIME
1 HOUR

Serves 2

VEGETARIAN

Congee, or rice porridge, comes in several different varieties, both sweet and savory. Sometimes it's cooked until it's smooth and silky; other times it's thicker and more rustic. If you prefer, you can leave the eggs whole rather than scrambling them, and poach them in the porridge before serving.

¼ cup Arborio rice (or long grain)

3 cups water

½ teaspoon kosher salt

2 eggs

1 tablespoon coarsely chopped fresh cilantro

1 tablespoon minced fresh chives

1 to 2 teaspoons hot chili oil or sesame oil (optional)

1. Place the rice in a strainer and rinse well. Add the rice, water, and salt to the Dutch oven and cover. Place over medium-high heat and bring to a boil. As soon as the water boils, reduce the heat to low and stir the mixture. Cover and simmer for about 45 minutes, stirring every 15 minutes or so to keep the rice from sticking. After 45 minutes, the rice should be very soft and the porridge should have a silky consistency. If not, cook for another 10 minutes or so.

2. While the porridge cooks, whisk together the two eggs in a small bowl.

3. When the rice is cooked, slowly pour the egg into the porridge in a thin stream. If you want a custardy texture, whisk the mixture quickly while you pour in the egg. If you prefer ribbons of egg, stir more slowly. Cook for a minute or two or until the egg is done.

4. Stir in the cilantro and chives, and drizzle over the oil (if using).

INGREDIENT TIP Medium-grain rice such as Arborio will render a more traditional texture, but long-grain rice works fine, too.

Breakfast Sausage and Cheddar Casserole

ACTIVE TIME
20 MINUTES

TOTAL TIME
2 HOURS
30 MINUTES
PLUS
REFRIGERATION
TIME

Serves 2

I call this "cheater's strata," because it's not layered the way a real strata is; it's more like a savory bread pudding. Not only is it faster and easier to assemble, it's just as delicious.

3 thick slices dense sandwich bread, cut into ¾- to 1-inch square pieces (about 3 cups)

1 to 2 tablespoons vegetable oil

½ pound bulk breakfast sausage

½ small onion, chopped (about ½ cup)

¼ small red or green bell pepper, chopped coarsely (about ⅓ cup)

1 cup milk

¼ cup heavy cream

3 eggs

¼ teaspoon kosher salt

4 ounces extra-sharp Cheddar cheese (about 1 cup), coarsely grated, divided

1. If the bread is fresh and soft, lay the cubes out on a sheet pan and allow to dry for 20 minutes or so.

2. Place the Dutch oven over medium heat. Add just enough oil to coat the bottom of the pot and add the sausage. Break the sausage into small chunks with a spatula or spoon and cook it until it starts to brown.

3. Add the onion and bell pepper and stir. Cook for another 5 minutes, or until the vegetables are softened and the sausage is browned. Take the pot off the heat and let the sausage mixture cool.

Depending on the sausage, you may have a layer of browned bits stuck to the bottom of the Dutch oven. If this is the case, you need to remove it so it doesn't burn during the final cooking. The easiest way to do this is to remove the sausage and onion mixture to a bowl while the pot is hot. Pour in ¼ cup white wine or water and deglaze the pot by scraping up the browned bits from the bottom. Let the liquid reduce to a couple of table-spoons, and add it to the milk mixture you make in step 4.

4. In a small bowl, whisk together the milk, cream, eggs, and salt until completely blended. Add the bread cubes to the sausage mixture in the Dutch oven along with half the Cheddar, and gently combine. Pour in the egg mixture. Cover the Dutch oven and refrigerate for 1 to 2 hours, up to overnight.

5. Preheat the oven to 350°F.

6. Uncover the Dutch oven and sprinkle the remaining Cheddar cheese over the casserole. Bake, uncovered, for about 30 minutes, or until puffed up and browned on the top. (If the casserole has been refrigerated overnight, add another 10 minutes or so to the baking time.)

TECHNIQUE TIP If you are planning to refrigerate the casserole overnight, cut the bread into the larger, 1-inch chunks. If you plan to bake it after 1 to 2 hours, use the smaller chunks.

Crustless Quiches with Bacon and Onions

ACTIVE TIME
15 MINUTES

TOTAL TIME
35 MINUTES

Serves 2

These quiches are assembled in ramekins that rest in the Dutch oven in very hot water, known as a water bath. With some toast and fresh fruit, these make a delicious light breakfast. If you prefer a larger serving, double the recipe, but cook in four small ramekins rather than a larger size so they cook quickly and evenly.

Vegetable oil or butter for coating ramekins

1 slice bacon, diced

½ very small onion, sliced thin (about ¼ cup)

½ teaspoon kosher salt, plus a pinch for seasoning

1 large egg plus 1 egg yolk

¼ cup whole milk

¼ cup heavy cream

Freshly ground black or white pepper

2 tablespoons shredded Swiss cheese

1. Preheat the oven to 350°F.

2. Coat the inside of two 1-cup ramekins with vegetable oil or very soft butter.

3. Place the Dutch oven over medium heat. Add the bacon. Cook, stirring occasionally, until the bacon has rendered most of its fat and is mostly crisp, 2 to 3 minutes. Add the onion and season with a pinch or two of kosher salt. Cook, stirring, until the onions just begin to brown, about 3 minutes. Remove the bacon and onions and drain briefly on paper towels.

4. Wipe out the inside of the Dutch oven. Set the empty ramekins in the Dutch oven and add enough water to come up to within ½ inch of the tops of the ramekins. Remove the ramekins and heat the water over medium-high heat just until simmering.

5. While the water heats, add the egg and yolk to a small bowl. Add the milk, cream, remaining ½ teaspoon of salt, and pepper and whisk until the mixture is well combined.

6. Divide the cheese, and the bacon and onion mixture among the ramekins. Pour the egg mixture over it.

7. When the water is just barely simmering, place the ramekins in the Dutch oven, then transfer to the oven. Bake the custards for 20 minutes, or until set (a skewer inserted into the center should come out clean).

8. Carefully remove the Dutch oven and then, using tongs, remove the ramekins from the water. Let cool for 5 to 10 minutes before serving.

TECHNIQUE TIP A Dutch oven may not be typically used for a water bath (or *bain-marie*), but it works quite well in that role. Not only can you heat the water on the stove before moving it to the oven, but since it's deep, you're less likely to spill the water as you're moving it.

Baked Oatmeal with Blueberries and Apples

ACTIVE TIME
20 MINUTES

TOTAL TIME
1 HOUR

Serves 2

VEGETARIAN

This version of oatmeal is more like a soft breakfast bar with fruit than porridge. It makes a good addition to a brunch or breakfast buffet.

1 to 2 tablespoons butter

½ Gala apple, peeled, cored and cut into ½-inch pieces

½ cup fresh blueberries

1 tablespoon maple syrup

⅔ cup uncooked rolled oats

¼ cup blanched slivered almonds

¼ teaspoon baking powder

¼ teaspoon cinnamon

Pinch kosher salt

⅔ cup whole milk

1 egg yolk

2 teaspoons brown sugar

¼ teaspoon vanilla extract

1. Preheat the oven to 375°F.

2. Butter the bottom of the Dutch oven and about 1 inch up the sides. Add the apple and blueberries in a thin layer. Drizzle with the maple syrup.

3. In a medium bowl, mix together the oats, almonds, baking powder, cinnamon, and salt.

4. In a small bowl, whisk together the milk, egg yolk, sugar, and vanilla and pour over the oat mixture. Stir just until combined and spoon over the fruit.

5. Bake, uncovered, for 30 to 35 minutes, or until the top is golden brown and the fruit is bubbling. Let cool for 10 to 15 minutes before serving.

SEASONAL SWAP You can use any fresh fruit in season, or your favorite frozen fruits (thawed and drained) in this dish.

Dutch Baby with Lemon Glaze

Somewhere between a pancake and popover, a Dutch baby (also known as a Finnish pancake) supposedly originated in Seattle, Washington. While I don't know if that's true, I got this recipe from my Mom during my high school years in the Seattle area. I've been making it ever since.

ACTIVE TIME
10 MINUTES

TOTAL TIME
35 MINUTES

Serves 2

VEGETARIAN

3 tablespoons unsalted butter

½ cup all-purpose flour

1 tablespoon granulated sugar

¼ teaspoon kosher salt

2 large eggs

½ cup whole milk

¼ teaspoon vanilla extract

½ lemon, juiced (about 1 tablespoon)

3 tablespoons confectioners' (powdered) sugar

1. Preheat the oven to 400°F.

2. Place the Dutch oven over medium heat and add the butter.

3. While the butter melts, make the batter. If you have a blender, add the flour, sugar, salt, eggs, milk, and vanilla to the jar and blend until smooth. If you don't, add the ingredients to a medium bowl and use a hand mixer to beat until smooth.

4. When the Dutch oven is hot on the sides and the butter has stopped foaming, pour in the batter and bake, uncovered, for 20 minutes without opening the oven. The pancake should be puffed and golden brown, with darker brown edges. Bake for another 5 minutes if necessary.

5. Drizzle with the lemon juice. Place the confectioner's sugar in a small fine sieve and sprinkle over the pancake.

Baked French Toast with Spiced Apples

ACTIVE TIME
30 MINUTES

TOTAL TIME
2 HOURS
PLUS
REFRIGERATION
TIME

Serves 2

VEGETARIAN

While this baked French toast doesn't share the crispness of the more traditional stove top version, it tastes just as decadent and delicious. Like the Breakfast Sausage and Cheddar Casserole (page 32), this dish can be prepared ahead of time and refrigerated overnight. The apples can be made the day before and reheated, so it makes a great lazy Sunday brunch entrée.

FOR THE SPICED APPLES

1 large Gala apple

2 tablespoons unsalted butter

3 tablespoons brown sugar

1 tablespoon apple brandy, Calvados, or regular brandy

¼ teaspoon ground cinnamon

Pinch ground cardamom

Pinch salt

FOR THE FRENCH TOAST

½ cup whole milk

⅓ cup heavy cream

1 egg plus 1 yolk

1 teaspoon maple syrup

¼ teaspoon vanilla extract

Pinch salt

4 small slices dry or stale dense bread, ½-inch thick

¼ cup granulated sugar

½ teaspoon ground cinnamon

⅛ teaspoon ground cardamom (optional)

1. Peel and core the apple. Cut into thin slices and then cut each slice into small pieces (about ½-inch squares). Melt the butter in the Dutch oven over medium heat. Add the apples, and stir to coat with the butter.

2. Add the brown sugar, brandy, cinnamon, cardamom, and salt and bring to a simmer. Cover and cook for about 20 minutes or so, stirring occasionally, until the apples are soft but not falling apart. Transfer from the Dutch oven to a bowl and let cool, then cover.

3. In a small bowl, whisk together the milk, cream, egg and yolk, maple syrup, vanilla, and salt until completely blended. Place the bread in the bottom of the Dutch oven and pour the egg mixture over it. Cover the Dutch oven and refrigerate for 2 hours, or up to overnight.

4. Preheat the oven to 375°F.

5. In a small bowl, whisk together the sugar, cinnamon, and cardamom (if using). Sprinkle the egg mixture in the Dutch oven with the cinnamon-sugar mixture.

6. Bake, uncovered, for about 30 minutes, or until puffed up and browned on the top. (If the French toast has been refrigerated overnight, add another 10 minutes or so to the baking time.)

7. While the French toast is baking, warm the apples in a small saucepan or in the microwave. Serve the French toast topped with the apples.

INGREDIENT TIP If you prefer not to make the apple topping, top the French toast with fresh berries, jam, or maple syrup.

SOUPS, CHOWDERS & CHILIS

chapter
three

Chicken and Rice Soup with Ginger Scallion Sauce

ACTIVE TIME
25 MINUTES

TOTAL TIME
25 MINUTES

Serves 2

The ginger-scallion sauce in this soup is my version of a recipe by David Chang of New York's Momofuku restaurants, which is his version of a sauce from a Chinatown noodle shop. You'll have extra sauce, but it's difficult to make a smaller amount. Use the leftover sauce on scrambled eggs or mixed into ramen or other noodle dishes. It will keep several days in the refrigerator.

FOR THE GINGER-SCALLION SAUCE

3 tablespoons peeled and minced ginger root (2- to 3-inch piece)

1 cup chopped scallions (about ½ bunch)

¼ teaspoon hoisin sauce

½ teaspoon sherry vinegar or rice vinegar

½ teaspoon soy sauce

1 tablespoon canola or other neutral vegetable oil

FOR THE SOUP

1 to 2 tablespoons vegetable oil

1 tablespoon finely minced garlic

1 tablespoon finely minced fresh ginger

2 tablespoons finely minced onion

3 cups low-sodium chicken stock

¼ teaspoon kosher salt

¼ cup long-grain rice

1 small carrot, peeled and cut into thin coins

1 small boneless chicken breast, cut into bite-size chunks

2 to 3 ounces sugar snap peas or snow peas, strings removed

½ cup frozen pearl onions, thawed

2 to 3 tablespoons ginger-scallion sauce

1. To make the ginger-scallion sauce, place the ginger in the bowl of a small food processor and process for 30 seconds or so. Add the scallions and continue to process for a minute until the vegetables form a coarse paste (don't over-process, or the scallions can become bitter).

2. Add the hoisin, vinegar, soy sauce, and oil, and process until the mixture is smoother but not completely puréed. If the mixture is too thick, add a teaspoon or two of water to thin it out. (If you don't have a small food processor, mince the ginger and scallions as fine as possible and stir in the rest of the ingredients.)

3. To make the soup, place the Dutch oven over medium heat. Add enough oil to coat the bottom of the pot and heat until the oil shimmers. Add the garlic, ginger, and onion and cook, stirring, until fragrant, about 2 minutes. Add the chicken stock and salt and bring to a simmer.

4. Pour in the rice and cover the pot. Cook for 7 minutes.

5. Add the carrot and chicken breast. Simmer for 5 minutes.

6. Add the peas and pearl onions, and simmer for another 3 minutes. Taste the rice; it should be soft but not mushy. If it's still hard in the center of a grain, simmer until tender. Adjust the seasoning, adding more salt if necessary.

7. Ladle the soup into two bowls and add about a tablespoon of ginger-scallion sauce to each bowl.

Italian Braised Celery Soup with Pancetta

ACTIVE TIME
20 MINUTES

TOTAL TIME
1 HOUR
10 MINUTES

Serves 2

When you're cooking for two, it can seem impossible to use up a whole head of celery before it starts to turn limp. This soup—based on a recipe for braised celery by the late Marcella Hazan, renowned Italian cookbook author—is a delicious change from the cream of celery soup you may have grown up with.

1 tablespoon olive oil

2 to 3 ounces pancetta, diced

1 small onion, sliced thin

1 garlic clove, minced

5 to 6 celery stalks, sliced into ¼-inch pieces (about 2 cups)

Kosher salt

⅓ cup dry white wine

2½ cups low-sodium chicken stock

¼ teaspoon red pepper flakes

⅔ cup diced tomatoes with their juice (about half a 15-ounce can)

Freshly ground black pepper

¼ cup celery leaves, roughly chopped (optional)

1. Place the Dutch oven over medium heat. Add enough oil to coat the bottom of the pot and heat until the oil shimmers. Add the pancetta and stir to break it up. Cook, stirring occasionally, until the pancetta crisps and renders most of its fat. If you like, remove a couple of tablespoons of the cooked pancetta and set aside to garnish the soup.

2. Add the onion, garlic, and celery to the Dutch oven and stir to coat the vegetables with the fat in the pot. Season with salt and lower the heat to medium-low. Cook, stirring occasionally, until the vegetables are softened slightly, about 4 minutes.

3. Add the wine and bring to a boil. Cook until most of the wine has evaporated and then add the chicken stock, red pepper flakes, and tomatoes. Adjust the heat to keep the soup at a low simmer, and cover.

4. Cook for 40 to 50 minutes, or until the celery is very tender. Season with salt and pepper. Garnish with the reserved pancetta and celery leaves (if using).

Chicken Sausage, Kale, and Cannellini Bean Soup

ACTIVE TIME
15 MINUTES

TOTAL TIME
40 MINUTES

Serves 2

This twist on Pasta e Fagioli combines chicken sausage with the pasta and beans, with a little kale. You can substitute other greens, or even broccoli rabe if you prefer.

1 tablespoon olive oil

½ pound mild or spicy Italian-style chicken sausage, casings removed

½ small onion, chopped (about ½ cup)

1 medium garlic clove, minced

3 cups low-sodium chicken stock

1 sprig fresh rosemary

1 (14-ounce) can cannellini beans, drained and rinsed

½ cup tiny shells, macaroni, or other very small pasta

½ small bunch kale, tough stems removed and cut into ½-inch ribbons (about 3 cups)

1 teaspoon red wine vinegar

¼ cup grated Parmigiano-Reggiano or similar cheese

1. Place the Dutch oven over medium heat. Add the olive oil and heat until it shimmers. Add the sausage, breaking it up into bite-size pieces. Cook until the pieces are browned on the outside, about 3 minutes.

2. Add the onion and cook, stirring, for a minute or two, just until the onion pieces begin to separate. Add the garlic and cook for a couple of minutes longer, or until fragrant.

3. Add the chicken stock and rosemary and bring to a simmer. Stir in the beans, pasta, and kale and bring back to a simmer. Cook, uncovered, for 20 minutes, stirring occasionally. Check the pasta to make sure it's done, and stir in the vinegar. Taste and adjust the seasoning, adding more vinegar if the soup needs brightening.

4. Ladle into bowls and serve with grated Parmigiano-Reggiano.

TECHNIQUE TIP This soup can easily be doubled and the extras frozen, but in that case, leave out the pasta. It gets mushy when frozen. You can either omit it entirely, or add it separately when ready to serve.

Mushroom and Shallot Soup with Chives

ACTIVE TIME
20 MINUTES

TOTAL TIME
45 MINUTES

Serves 2

VEGETARIAN

This cooking method is a little different from what you might expect: The mushrooms are covered with water and brought to a boil. They cook thoroughly as the water evaporates, and are then browned in the butter that remains in the bottom of the pan. It results in mushrooms with a very concentrated flavor. It couldn't be easier, as the only time you need to attend to the mushrooms is when they begin to brown at the very end.

1 pound cremini or white button mushrooms

3 tablespoons butter, cut into 3 pieces

Kosher salt

¼ cup dried porcini mushrooms

1 large shallot, sliced thin

⅓ cup dry or medium dry sherry

2½ cups low-sodium vegetable stock

¼ cup heavy cream

Freshly ground black pepper

1 tablespoon minced chives

1. Wash the mushrooms and trim the stems, reserving them for later. Quarter the mushrooms if small to medium; cut into eighths if they are large. Pile the mushrooms in the Dutch oven and cover with just enough water to make the mushrooms float. Add the butter chunks and sprinkle generously with salt. Place the pot over high heat and bring to a boil. Continue boiling until the water has all evaporated and you can hear the mushrooms begin to sizzle; this can take from 12 to 20 minutes, depending on the amount of water and pan size.

2. While the mushrooms cook, measure out ½ cup of the hottest possible tap water into a measuring cup and add the dried porcini mushrooms. Let them soak for at least 15 minutes, pushing them down into the water a few times to make sure they soak and don't float.

3. When the mushrooms in the Dutch oven start to sizzle, turn them a few times with a spatula to brown them on several sides. Remove about half of them and set aside.

4. Add the shallot and the reserved mushroom stems. Sprinkle with salt and cook, stirring occasionally, until softened, about 5 minutes. Add the sherry and bring to a strong simmer. Cook, stirring occasionally, for 5 to 7 minutes, until most of the wine evaporates.

5. While the sherry reduces, strain the dried mushrooms from the hot water, filtering out any grit or sand that may accumulate at the bottom, and discard the grit and mushrooms. Add the mushroom water, vegetable stock, and about half the reserved cooked mushrooms, and simmer, covered, for 20 minutes.

6. If you have an immersion blender, blend the soup until the texture is as smooth as you like it. (If you don't have an immersion blender, pour the mixture into a blender or food processor and pulse to get the desired texture. Pour the soup back into the Dutch oven.) Add the remaining mushrooms and the cream. Heat to a simmer, season with black pepper, and add half the chives. Taste and adjust the seasoning.

7. Ladle into bowls and garnish with the remaining chives.

INGREDIENT TIP For this recipe, try to find a brand of vegetable stock that lists mushrooms as one of the first ingredients, so you get more mushroom flavor. I like Kitchen Basics brand.

Creamy Carrot Soup with Garlic and Cumin

ACTIVE TIME
20 MINUTES

TOTAL TIME
45 MINUTES

Serves 2

VEGETARIAN

The earthy flavor of carrots matches well with any number of flavorings, from herbs like parsley or chives, to ginger or allspice or even vanilla. I especially like them with cumin, a combination I first tried in a Turkish carrot salad. The cumin contrasts nicely with the sweetness of the carrots, and the pinch of cayenne and garlic add depth. Don't worry about the large amount of garlic. It becomes mild and sweet as it cooks.

1 tablespoon unsalted butter

½ small onion, coarsely chopped (about ⅓ cup)

4 large garlic cloves, smashed and peeled

½ pound carrots, peeled and cut into coins

¼ teaspoon kosher salt, plus more for seasoning

¼ cup dry or medium dry sherry

2 cups low-sodium vegetable broth

⅛ teaspoon ground cumin (or more for seasoning)

Pinch cayenne pepper

¼ cup fresh or pasteurized carrot juice

1 tablespoon heavy cream

1. Melt the butter in the Dutch oven over medium-low heat. When the butter stops foaming, add the onion and garlic and cook, stirring, for a few minutes until the onion pieces separate and begin to soften. Add the carrots and salt. Cook for about 6 minutes, stirring until the vegetables begin to brown.

2. Turn the heat to medium-high and add the sherry. Bring it to a boil and cook for a couple of minutes, until mostly evaporated. Add the vegetable broth and bring to a simmer. Cover and cook for 25 to 30 minutes, or until the carrots are very soft.

3. Transfer the soup to a blender and carefully purée until smooth, working in batches if necessary. You can also use an immersion blender, although in my experience it doesn't get the soup as smooth as I like. Return to the Dutch oven and place back over low heat.

4. Add the cumin, cayenne, carrot juice, and cream and bring to a simmer. Adjust the seasoning, adding salt as necessary.

INGREDIENT TIP I like this soup as an accompaniment to a plate of cheese, sausages, olives, and country bread. A crisp white wine like a Sauvignon Blanc is the perfect complement.

Broccoli Soup with Aged Cheddar and Almonds

ACTIVE TIME
25 MINUTES

TOTAL TIME
25 MINUTES

Serves 2

I developed this recipe for a class focused on healthy versions of dishes that are normally higher in fat and calories. Without lots of cream, the broccoli flavor shines, but a touch of aged Cheddar and toasted almonds add depth of flavor and texture. Because there's not very much cheese in the soup, it's important to use one that packs a punch. Look for a cheese that's been aged at least 18 months.

2 tablespoons butter

1 small onion, thinly sliced

¼ teaspoon Kosher salt

¼ cup dry white wine

2½ cups low-sodium chicken stock

8 ounces broccoli florets

1 teaspoon Dijon mustard

⅛ teaspoon celery seed

⅛ teaspoon freshly ground white pepper

1 ounce coarsely shredded or crumbled aged Cheddar cheese

1 tablespoon sliced almonds, toasted until golden brown

1. Place the Dutch oven over medium heat and add the butter. When the butter stops foaming, add the onion and season with salt. Stir until the onions are coated with the butter. Cook for about 5 minutes, stirring occasionally, until softened.

2. Add the wine and bring to a simmer. Cook, stirring occasionally, for a couple of minutes, until most of the wine evaporates.

3. Add the chicken stock and broccoli and simmer, covered, for an additional 5 minutes. Uncover the pan and continue to simmer until the broccoli is tender, 2 to 3 more minutes. Remove from the heat and let cool slightly.

4. If you have an immersion blender, blend the soup until the texture is as smooth as you like it. (If you don't have an immersion blender, pour the mixture into a blender or food processor and pulse to get the desired texture. Pour the soup back into the Dutch oven.) Add the mustard, celery seed, and pepper. Taste and add more salt if necessary.

5. To serve, put the cheese in a bowl and pour the soup over. Top with the almonds.

INGREDIENT TIP Garnishing the soup with a few small blanched broccoli florets adds visual interest and more texture to the soup. If you want, reserve a few of the very tiny top florets as a garnish. To prepare the broccoli, bring a cup or so of water to a boil in a small saucepan; add 1 teaspoon or so of salt. As soon as the water boils, add the small florets and cook for 2 minutes. Remove and drain.

Tortilla Soup

ACTIVE TIME
25 MINUTES

TOTAL TIME
40 MINUTES

Serves 2

Tortilla soup is a wonderful way to use up old tortillas and make a meal from simple ingredients, in this case broth and tomatoes. Like many peasant dishes, it can get fancier and more substantial. This version contains chicken and is garnished with cheese and avocado, but it still comes together quickly. Use cooked shredded chicken to speed it up even more.

2 to 3 cups vegetable oil

2 to 3 corn tortillas, cut into ½-inch strips

Fine salt for the tortilla strips

½ small onion, finely chopped

1 small jalapeño pepper, seeded and minced

1 cup fire-roasted diced tomatoes in juice

1 large garlic clove, minced

3 cups low-sodium chicken stock

1 small boneless skinless chicken breast, cut into ½-inch chunks

2 tablespoons chopped fresh cilantro

1 teaspoon freshly squeezed lime juice

½ ripe avocado, pitted and diced

¼ cup shredded Monterey Jack cheese

1. Pour the oil into the Dutch oven and place over medium-high heat. Heat the oil to 350°F to 375°F. When the oil is hot, carefully add a layer of tortilla strips; don't crowd the pan. Cook for 5 minutes or so, separating and turning as necessary, until deep golden brown and crisp. Remove from the oil and drain on a fine grid rack set over a sheet pan, or on paper towels. (If you use paper towels, remove the chips from the towels as soon as they're drained so they don't reabsorb the oil from the towels.) Sprinkle lightly with salt. Repeat with the remaining tortilla strips. Pour out all but a light coating of the oil.

2. Place the Dutch oven over medium heat until the oil shimmers. Add the onion and jalapeño and let them cook without stirring for 4 to 5 minutes, or until they begin to brown. Stir in the tomatoes and garlic, and bring to a simmer. Cook for about 15 minutes, or until the mixture has thickened and the vegetables are soft.

3. Break up the tomato mixture into a chunky paste with a potato masher or a large fork. Add the chicken stock and bring to a simmer. Add the chicken breast and cover. Cook for 8 to 12 minutes, or until the chicken is cooked. Stir in the cilantro and lime juice and taste, adding more salt if necessary.

4. Divide the avocado and cheese between two bowls and ladle the soup over. Top with the tortilla strips.

Short Rib Soup with Caramelized Onions

ACTIVE TIME
30 MINUTES

TOTAL TIME
4 HOURS

Serves 2

Several years ago, I tried a dish simply called "short rib soup" at an Atlanta restaurant. After my first bite, I thought, "This is what French onion soup dreams of being." Not that there's anything wrong with French onion soup, but the short rib soup was deeper, more complex, and absolutely delicious. This is my version. It takes a long time, so it's definitely a weekend project, but it can be done in stages.

4 tablespoons butter, divided

5 to 6 medium white or yellow onions, sliced thin (about 6 cups), divided

Kosher salt

1 pound bone-in short ribs

⅓ cup dry or medium-dry sherry

2½ cups low-sodium beef stock

¼ teaspoon dried thyme (or 1 sprig fresh)

1 bay leaf

1 teaspoon Worcestershire sauce

1 teaspoon sherry vinegar (optional)

1. To make the caramelized onions, place the Dutch oven over medium heat. Add half the butter and melt until it starts to foam. Add about 4 cups of the onions and stir to coat with the butter. Season with salt and cover. Turn the heat down to low. Cook for at least an hour (usually 90 minutes), stirring every 15 minutes or so. The onions will soften, then slowly turn golden and then light amber in color. There should still be a fair amount of liquid in the pot. This process can take longer depending on the moisture level of the onions; be patient and don't try to hasten the process by turning up the heat or you risk burning them.

2. Uncover and turn the heat up to medium. Cook the onions, stirring occasionally, until they darken to a deep caramel color and the liquid has evaporated and about ⅔ cup of onions remains. Transfer the caramelized onions to a bowl and set aside.

3. While the onions cook, salt the short ribs on all sides. Turn the heat to medium-high and add the rest of the butter to the Dutch oven. When the butter stops foaming, add the remaining sliced onions and stir. Spread them into a single layer, and cook without stirring until they start to brown, 2 to 4 minutes. Stir, and repeat the process, until the onions are mostly browned. Transfer to a bowl and set aside. These onions should be browned but not caramelized.

4. Place the short ribs in the Dutch oven and cook for several minutes, or until browned. Repeat until all sides are brown; about 12 to 15 minutes. Transfer the short ribs to a plate.

5. Add the sherry to the pot and bring to a simmer, scraping up the browned bits from the bottom. Cook until the sherry has reduced by about half then add the beef stock, thyme, and bay leaf. Stir in the caramelized onions, reserving the browned onions. Add the short ribs and bring the mixture to a simmer.

6. Cover and simmer gently for at least 90 minutes and up to 2 hours, turning the short ribs halfway through. When the meat is tender, remove the ribs and let them cool. Remove the bay leaf and thyme sprig and discard. Strain out the onions and reserve.

7. From the surface of the mixture sauce, skim off as much fat as possible and add the caramelized onions back to the soup. Bring to a simmer.

8. When the ribs have cooled enough to handle, shred the meat, discarding the bones, tendons, and any remaining fat. Add the meat to the soup along with the browned onions and the Worcestershire sauce. Taste and add salt if necessary. If the soup seems too sweet, add the optional sherry vinegar.

TECHNIQUE TIP You can make the caramelized onions ahead of time for this recipe or any others. Refrigerate them for up to 3 days or move them to the freezer.

VG+ to excellent

West African Peanut Soup with Chicken

ACTIVE TIME
15 MINUTES

TOTAL TIME
1 HOUR

Serves 2

This is one rich, hearty, and deliciously sweet and savory meal. I prefer to keep both the chicken and sweet potatoes chunky, which makes it a bit more stew-like.

1 to 2 tablespoons vegetable or olive oil

½ small onion, sliced thin

1 large garlic clove, minced

1 teaspoon minced or grated ginger

Kosher salt

¼ teaspoon red pepper flakes

3 cups low-sodium chicken stock

1 (14-ounce) can diced tomatoes, drained

1 to 2 boneless skinless chicken thighs, cut into bite-size pieces

1 very small sweet potato, peeled and cut into ½-inch chunks

¼ cup peanut butter

1 to 2 tablespoons chopped roasted unsalted peanuts

1. Place the Dutch oven over medium heat. Add enough oil to coat the bottom of the pot and heat until the oil shimmers. Add the onion and stir to coat with the oil. Cook, stirring, for a minute or two, just until the onion pieces begin to separate. Add the garlic and ginger and sprinkle with salt. Cook, stirring, for a couple of minutes, or until fragrant. Add the red pepper flakes, chicken stock, and diced tomatoes and bring to a simmer. Cover and cook for about 20 minutes.

2. Add the chicken and sweet potato chunks to the mixture. Bring the soup back to a simmer and cover. Cook for another 20 to 25 minutes, or until the sweet potatoes are soft.

3. Stir in the peanut butter, and taste for seasoning. Ladle into bowls and sprinkle with chopped peanuts.

INGREDIENT TIP Some recipes for the soup include kale in addition to the sweet potato. If you like, add a few sliced kale leaves with the chicken and sweet potato.

North African Chickpea Stew

Dutch ovens are perfect for slow cooking dried beans such as chickpeas. Soaking them cuts down on the cooking time and results in more even cooking. This stew, with spices typical in North African cuisine, is deeply flavored. If you happen to have a jar of preserved lemons, mince about a tablespoon and use in place of the lemon zest. Preserved lemons often garnish North African dishes.

ACTIVE TIME
15 MINUTES

TOTAL TIME
1 HOUR
10 MINUTES
PLUS
SOAKING TIME

Serves 2

VEGAN

Kosher salt

¼ pound dried chickpeas

½ small onion, diced

1 medium garlic clove, minced or pressed

½ teaspoon ground coriander

¼ teaspoon ground cumin

¼ teaspoon freshly ground black pepper

⅛ teaspoon ground cinnamon

⅛ teaspoon red pepper flakes

1 small carrot, peeled and cut into thin coins

1 small tomato, seeded and diced

2 cups fresh baby spinach or arugula

1 teaspoon lemon zest

1 tablespoon minced fresh parsley

1. Dissolve 1 tablespoon salt in 1 quart of water, in a large bowl. Add the chickpeas and soak at room temperature for 8 to 24 hours. Drain and rinse the chickpeas.

2. Add the chickpeas, onion, garlic, coriander, cumin, pepper, cinnamon, and red pepper flakes to the Dutch oven and add 4 cups of fresh water. Place over high heat and bring to a boil. Reduce the heat to medium-low and simmer for 45 minutes, or until the chickpeas are almost tender.

3. Add the carrot and tomato and simmer for another 10 minutes, or until the carrots and chickpeas are tender. (If the broth is too thin, bring it back to a boil and reduce until thickened.) Stir in the spinach or arugula and cook until wilted, about 1 minute.

4. Ladle into two bowls and garnish with the lemon zest and parsley.

Manhattan Clam Chowder

Red clam chowder with tomatoes comes not from Manhattan but from Rhode Island, or so the story goes. With lots of vegetables and without the creamy base, it's a lighter soup than its New England relative. This clam chowder, regardless of where it originated, makes a satisfying light dinner with a few slices of crusty bread.

2 pounds medium hard-shelled clams (cherrystones), scrubbed well

2 bacon slices, diced

½ small onion, chopped (about ½ cup)

¼ medium green bell pepper, chopped (about ⅓ cup)

½ small rib celery, chopped (about ¼ cup)

½ medium carrot, peeled and chopped (about ¼ cup)

Kosher salt

1 medium Yukon Gold potato, peeled and diced (generous 1 cup)

1 (8-ounce) bottle clam juice

1 bay leaf

¼ teaspoon dried thyme (or 1 sprig fresh)

¼ teaspoon red pepper flakes

1 (14-ounce) can diced tomatoes, drained

2 tablespoons chopped fresh parsley, for garnish

1. Add 2 cups of water to a Dutch oven and place over medium-high heat. When the water comes to a boil, add the clams and cover the pot. Cook for 10 minutes, then uncover the pot and stir the clams. Cook for another 5 minutes or so, or until the clams have opened. Discard any that haven't opened. Transfer the clams to a shallow bowl and let them cool. Strain the liquid through a fine strainer lined with cheesecloth or paper towels, and set aside.

2. Wipe out the Dutch oven and place it over medium heat. Add the diced bacon. Cook, stirring occasionally, until the bacon has rendered most of its fat and is mostly crisp, 3 to 5 minutes. Remove the bacon and set aside, leaving the fat in the pot.

3. Add the onion, bell pepper, celery, and carrot and sprinkle with a pinch or two of kosher salt. Cook, stirring, until the vegetables soften, about 4 minutes.

4. Add the potato, bottled clam juice, reserved clam liquid, bay leaf, thyme, red pepper flakes, and tomatoes. Bring the soup to a simmer and cover. Reduce the heat to medium-low to maintain a simmer and cook for 25 minutes, or until the potatoes are soft.

5. While the soup cooks, remove the clams from their shells and chop into ½-inch pieces (if small, this might not be necessary). When the soup has simmered long enough, remove the bay leaf and thyme stem (if you've used fresh thyme). Stir in the clams to heat through, about 3 minutes.

6. Ladle into bowls and garnish with the reserved bacon and the parsley.

INGREDIENT TIP If you can't find clam juice, you can substitute tomato-clam juice, such as Clamato, or seafood stock.

Southwestern Corn and Poblano Chowder

ACTIVE TIME
20 MINUTES

TOTAL TIME
45 MINUTES

Serves 2

VEGETARIAN

I got the idea for this soup from the Mexican dish called *rajas*, which is roasted poblano peppers and onions in a cream sauce, served as a side dish or a taco filling. Corn and chiles seemed like a natural match, so I was only a potato away from chowder. Serve the soup with warm, buttered corn or flour tortillas.

2 medium poblano chiles

2 to 3 tablespoons olive oil

½ small onion, sliced thin

Kosher salt

2 cups whole milk

¼ cup heavy cream

1 medium Yukon Gold potato, peeled and diced in ½-inch cubes

¼ teaspoon ground cumin

¼ teaspoon ancho chili powder

½ cup frozen corn kernels, thawed

⅛ teaspoon Mexican hot sauce, such as Valentina (optional)

1 teaspoon freshly squeezed lime juice (optional)

1 tablespoon chopped fresh cilantro, for garnish

1. Set the broiler on high, with the rack in the highest position. Place the poblanos, skin-side up, on a broiler pan or baking sheet and broil until they're blackened and the skin puffs. Place them in a bowl and cover for 10 to 15 minutes. Peel the skin off and cut the pieces into small chunks.

2. While the poblanos are steaming, place the Dutch oven over medium heat. Add enough oil to coat the bottom of the pot and heat until the oil shimmers and flows like water. Add the onion and sprinkle with salt. Cook, stirring, for 3 to 5 minutes, or until the onion pieces separate and soften.

3. Add the milk, cream, potato, cumin, and chili powder. Bring to a simmer and cook, uncovered, for 15 to 18 minutes, or until the potatoes are just tender. Add the poblano chiles and corn, and bring back to a simmer. Cook for 10 minutes and taste, adjusting the seasoning. Season with hot sauce and lime juice (if using).

4. Ladle into bowls and garnish with the cilantro.

Black Bean and Corn Chili

Chili is perfect for eating on a cool night, curled up in front of the television. It cooks up quickly because of the canned beans, and clean-up is easy, too. Consider making a double batch, as leftovers freeze well.

ACTIVE TIME
30 MINUTES

TOTAL TIME
30 MINUTES

Serves 2

VEGETARIAN

2 to 3 tablespoons vegetable oil

½ small onion, diced

2 medium garlic cloves, minced

½ small red or green bell pepper, seeded and diced

Kosher salt

2 tablespoons ancho chili powder

1 teaspoon ground cumin

½ teaspoon dried oregano

½ cup diced canned tomatoes with their juice

1 small chipotle chile in adobo, minced, plus 2 teaspoons of the adobo sauce

1 (14-ounce) can black beans, drained and rinsed

1 cup frozen corn kernels, thawed

½ avocado, diced

¼ cup shredded Monterey Jack cheese

2 scallions, diced

1. Place the Dutch oven over medium heat. Add enough oil to coat the bottom of the pot and heat until the oil shimmers. Add the onion, garlic, and bell pepper and season with salt. Cook, stirring, for 4 to 6 minutes, or until browned slightly.

2. Stir in the ancho chili powder, cumin, and oregano and cook for a minute or so, until the spices become fragrant. Add the tomatoes and bring to a simmer, scraping up any browned bits from the bottom of the pot.

3. Stir in the chipotle, black beans, and corn. Bring to a simmer and cover. Cook for about 15 minutes then uncover the pot. Continue to simmer until the sauce thickens. Taste and adjust the seasoning.

4. Ladle into bowls and top with the avocado, cheese, and scallions.

INGREDIENT TIP If you can't find pure ancho chili powder, you can use another chili powder. Add it before the other seasonings and adjust to taste.

Texas Chili

ACTIVE TIME
30 MINUTES

TOTAL TIME
90 MINUTES

Serves 2

Whether you call it Texas Chili, Chili Colorado, or Chile con Carne, this is the purist's version with meat only. Don't use a chili powder blend for this recipe; if you can't find ground ancho chili powder, use another type as long as it contains nothing but ground chiles.

1 pound beef shoulder (chuck), trimmed of fat and cut into ¾-inch cubes, divided

Kosher salt

2 to 3 tablespoons olive or vegetable oil

1 medium onion, sliced thin

2 garlic cloves, minced

2 tablespoons ancho chili powder

1 teaspoon ground cumin

½ teaspoon dried oregano

¼ teaspoon freshly ground black pepper

½ cup mild beer, such as lager

1½ cups low-sodium beef or chicken stock

¼ cup tomato sauce

1 chipotle chile in adobo sauce, minced, plus 2 teaspoons adobo sauce

1. Liberally season the beef cubes with salt.

2. Place the Dutch oven over medium heat. Add enough oil to coat the bottom of the pot and heat until the oil shimmers. Add half the beef cubes in a single layer and cook for 2 to 3 minutes, without stirring, until the first side is browned. Turn and brown at least one other side of the cubes. Transfer the beef to a plate.

3. Add the onion and garlic and cook, stirring, for 4 to 6 minutes, or until browned slightly. Stir in the ancho chili powder, cumin, oregano, and pepper and cook for a minute or so, until the spices become fragrant.

4. Pour in the beer and bring to a simmer, scraping up any browned bits from the bottom of the pot. Reduce by about half, then add the stock, tomato sauce, chipotle, and adobo sauce. Add the seared and raw beef and stir to coat. Bring the liquid to a simmer.

5. Cover and reduce the heat to simmer over medium-low. Cook for 45 to 60 minutes, stirring occasionally.

6. After 45 minutes, check a piece of beef. The beef should be tender enough to cut with a fork; if not, cook for another 15 to 20 minutes.

7. When the beef is tender, uncover and let it cool for 15 minutes to let any fat rise to the surface. Spoon or blot it off. Bring the chili back to a simmer to reduce the sauce slightly, until it's the consistency of gravy. Serve with chopped onions, grated cheese, or sour cream, if desired.

INGREDIENT TIP If you want beans in your chili, add a 14-ounce can of drained rinsed pintos after you've defatted the sauce. Simmer for 5 to 10 minutes to heat them through. With the beans, you'll probably have enough chili to freeze some for later.

Pork and White Bean Chili

ACTIVE TIME
25 MINUTES

TOTAL TIME
1 HOUR
30 MINUTES

Serves 2

Of the three chili recipes in this chapter, this is the least traditional. It's brothier than the other two, and although it contains plenty of chiles, it's got less chili powder, so lacks the "bowl of red" color many people associate with chili. Try it when you're in the mood for a milder but no less tasty chili.

1 large or 2 small Anaheim or other mild green chiles, seeded and cut into 3 or 4 fairly flat pieces

1 jalapeño pepper, seeded and cut into 3 or 4 fairly flat pieces

1 to 2 tablespoons vegetable or olive oil

⅔ cup frozen corn kernels, thawed

Kosher salt

½ small onion, coarsely chopped

1 small carrot, peeled and coarsely chopped

1 cup low-sodium chicken stock

1 teaspoon ground cumin

2 teaspoons ancho chili powder

¼ teaspoon chipotle powder or cayenne pepper

½ pound boneless country-style pork shoulder ribs, trimmed of fat and cut into bite-size pieces

1 (14-ounce) can cannellini beans, drained and rinsed

2 tablespoons chopped cilantro leaves

2 tablespoons sour cream

1. Set the broiler on high, with the rack in the highest position. Place the Anaheim chiles and jalapeño skin-side up on a broiler pan or baking sheet, and broil until they're blackened and their skin puffs. Place in a bowl and cover for 10 to 15 minutes. Peel the skin off and dice.

2. While the chiles cool, place the Dutch oven over medium-high heat. Add enough oil to coat the bottom of the pot and heat until the oil shimmers. Add the corn in a single layer and let it cook without stirring for 4 to 5 minutes, or until the corn starts to char. Sprinkle with salt and stir quickly. Pat the corn into a single layer again and let that side brown, 2 to 3 minutes. Turn the heat down to medium.

3. Add the onion and carrot and cook for 2 to 3 minutes, or until the onions just start to brown. Add the chicken stock and stir, scraping the bottom of the pot to get up any browned bits.

4. Season with salt, and add the cumin, ancho chili powder, and chipotle or cayenne. Bring to a simmer over medium-low heat and add the pork. Cover and cook for 30 minutes, adjusting the heat to keep the mixture at a simmer. Add the beans and cook for another 15 to 20 minutes, or until the pork is tender. Ladle into bowls and garnish with the sour cream and cilantro.

INGREDIENT TIP If you would rather, use cooked shredded pork or even chicken instead of the ribs. Skip the first cooking period, and add the cooked meat with the beans.

VEGETARIAN

chapter four

Sautéed Chard with
Cannellini Beans *68*

Mexican Red Rice and Beans *70*

Summer Succotash Bake *71*

Eggplant Parmesan *72*

Ratatouille with Navy Beans *74*

Oven Risotto with
Butternut Squash *76*

Sofrito and Gruyère-Stuffed
Portobello Mushrooms *78*

Three Cheese-Mushroom
Pasta Bake *80*

Penne Arrabiata *82*

Macaroni and Cheese with
Roasted Red Peppers and
Caramelized Onions *84*

Vegetable Korma *87*

Spiced Lentils and
Rice with Kale *88*

Masoor Dal *90*

Spicy Garlic Tofu with
Cashews and Spinach *92*

Sautéed Chard with Cannellini Beans

ACTIVE TIME
20 MINUTES

TOTAL TIME
40 MINUTES

Serves 2

VEGAN

Combining greens, especially chard, with beans is common in Italian cuisine. The combination is served alone, or with pasta for a more substantial dish. Most recipes call for discarding the stems of the chard, which I think is a mistake. While the stems do require longer cooking than the leaves, they have a nice flavor and when sautéed separately, can add a nice crunch to the softer cooked leaves.

1 bunch red or rainbow chard

2 to 3 tablespoons olive oil

½ small onion, chopped

2 garlic cloves, chopped

Kosher salt

¼ cup dry white wine

1 medium tomato, seeded and diced

2 tablespoons diced or puréed sun-dried tomatoes

¼ teaspoon red pepper flakes

1 (14-ounce) can cannellini beans, drained and rinsed

1. Rinse the chard and cut the leaves from the stems. Dice enough of the stems to make ½ cup; reserve the rest for another use or discard. Stack the leaves up and cut into ½-inch ribbons.

2. Place the Dutch oven over medium heat and add the olive oil. Heat until the oil shimmers and then add the onion, garlic, and chard stems. Season with salt and cook, stirring, for 5 to 6 minutes, or until the onion pieces have separated and the chard has softened.

3. Add the wine and bring to a simmer. Add the diced tomato, sun-dried tomatoes, and red pepper flakes.

4. Add the chard leaves by big handfuls, stirring to wilt. When all the chard is added, bring to a simmer and cover the Dutch oven. Cook for about 15 minutes, or until the chard is very soft. Taste and adjust the seasoning, adding more salt or red pepper flakes if necessary. Add the beans and cook for another 5 minutes, or until the beans are heated through.

INGREDIENT TIP Chard and beans are delicious ladled into bowls and topped with Parmigiano-Reggiano. For a more substantial dish, serve this over polenta.

Mexican Red Rice and Beans

ACTIVE TIME
20 MINUTES

TOTAL TIME
55 MINUTES

Serves 2

VEGAN

In my search for delicious Mexican red rice, also known as Spanish rice, I tried a couple of recipes, one from author and restaurateur Rick Bayless, and another from writer Sandra Gutierrez, who specializes in Latin American cuisine. This recipe borrows elements from both of them. I add beans to create a hearty vegan Mexican-inspired main dish.

2 to 3 tablespoons olive oil

½ small onion, chopped (about ⅓ cup)

1 large garlic clove, minced

1 small jalapeño pepper, seeded and chopped (about 1 tablespoon)

½ cup long-grain white rice

3 tablespoons red salsa

2 tablespoons tomato sauce

¾ cup vegetable stock

¼ teaspoon ground cumin

½ teaspoon kosher salt

1 (14-ounce) can pinto beans, drained and rinsed

1 tablespoon chopped fresh parsley

1. Preheat the oven to 350°F.

2. Place the Dutch oven over medium heat. Add enough oil to coat the bottom of the pot and heat until the oil shimmers. Add the onion, garlic, and jalapeño and cook, stirring, for 4 to 5 minutes, or until the onion pieces have separated and the vegetables have softened. Add the rice and stir to coat. Cook for about 1 minute.

3. Add the salsa, tomato sauce, vegetable stock, cumin, salt, and beans and stir to combine. Bring the liquid to a strong simmer and cover the Dutch oven.

4. Place the pot in the oven and cook for 18 minutes. Remove from the oven and let sit, covered, for 15 minutes. Remove the lid and add the parsley. Gently toss the rice with two large forks to fluff the rice and mix in the parsley.

Summer Succotash Bake

Succotash, at its most basic, is simply lima beans and corn. This recipe adds aromatics like onion and bell pepper to enliven the flavor. The addition of rice turns a side dish into a main dish casserole perfect for serving at a potluck or buffet.

ACTIVE TIME
15 MINUTES

TOTAL TIME
50 MINUTES

Serves 2

VEGAN

2 to 3 tablespoons olive oil

1 garlic clove, minced

½ medium green bell pepper, seeded and diced (about ½ cup)

½ small onion, chopped

⅓ cup long-grain rice

⅔ cup frozen lima beans, thawed

⅔ cup fresh or frozen (thawed) corn kernels

1 bay leaf

¼ teaspoon cayenne pepper

½ teaspoon Old Bay seasoning

⅔ cup low-sodium vegetable stock

¼ teaspoon kosher salt

1 large tomato, seeded and chopped

¼ cup chopped fresh parsley or basil, or a combination

1. Preheat the oven to 350°F.

2. Place the Dutch oven over medium heat. Add enough oil to coat the bottom of the pot and heat until the oil shimmers. Add the garlic, bell pepper, and onion and cook, stirring, for 4 to 5 minutes, or until the onion pieces have separated and softened. Add the rice and stir to coat with oil. Cook for about 1 minute. Stir in the lima beans, corn, bay leaf, cayenne, and Old Bay seasoning.

3. Add the vegetable stock and salt and stir to combine. Bring the liquid to a strong simmer and cover the Dutch oven. Place the pot in the oven and cook for 18 minutes.

4. Remove the pot from the oven and rest, covered, for 15 minutes. Taste the rice to make sure it's done. Fluff the rice mixture and stir in the tomatoes and parsley or basil. Rest for a few more minutes to warm the tomatoes through.

Eggplant Parmesan

This version of Eggplant Parmesan will win everyone over. It's all about the eggplant; I keep it crisp with panko and only a light coating of sauce and cheese. It's fresher, lighter, and even more delicious than the heavier ones you may have had in the past.

FOR THE EGGPLANT

1 medium eggplant (about 1 pound), sliced about ½-inch thick

Kosher salt

⅓ cup all-purpose flour

1 egg, whisked with 1 tablespoon water or milk

⅔ cup panko bread crumbs

½ teaspoon dried Italian herbs (or a mix of thyme, basil, and oregano)

½ cup grated Parmigiano-Reggiano or similar cheese, divided

Vegetable oil for frying

¼ cup shredded whole milk mozzarella cheese (or more)

FOR THE SAUCE

2 tablespoons olive oil

½ small onion, chopped

1 large garlic clove, minced

1 (14-ounce) can diced tomatoes, with their juice

2 tablespoons diced sun-dried tomatoes (optional)

¼ teaspoon dried Italian herbs

¼ teaspoon kosher salt

1. Place the eggplant slices on a rack set over a sheet pan. Season heavily with salt. Carefully turn the slices over and salt the other side. Set aside for 15 minutes while you prepare the breading.

2. In a shallow bowl, place the flour; in another shallow bowl, place the egg. In a third bowl, stir together the panko, Italian herbs, and ¼ cup of grated Parmigiano-Reggiano.

3. Place the Dutch oven over medium-high heat. Add enough oil to form a ½-inch layer in the bottom of the pot and heat until the oil reaches about 360°F.

4. While the oil heats, rinse off the eggplant slices with water and blot dry on both sides with paper towels. Working with a few slices at a time, dredge both sides of the eggplant slices in the flour, then coat with the egg. Place slices in the panko mixture and coat both sides.

5. When the oil is hot, carefully place the slices in the oil and fry for 2 to 3 minutes or until golden brown. Turn the slices over and cook for 2 minutes or until the second side is browned. Work in batches until all slices are browned. As the slices finish frying, move them to a rack placed over a sheet pan.

6. Preheat the oven to 375°F.

7. Pour the frying oil out of the Dutch oven (no need to wipe it out).

8. For the sauce, place the pot over medium heat and add the olive oil. Heat until the oil shimmers, and then add the onion and garlic. Cook, stirring, for 4 to 6 minutes, or until the onion pieces have separated and softened and the garlic is very fragrant.

9. Add the canned tomatoes with their juice, the sun-dried tomatoes (if using), and Italian herbs; bring to a simmer. Add the salt (slightly more if you're not using the sun-dried tomatoes) and stir. Bring to a simmer and cook for about 10 minutes. Using a potato masher or the back of a spoon, crush the tomatoes to form a smooth sauce. Taste and adjust the seasoning. Remove about ½ cup of the sauce.

10. Remove from the heat and use tongs to place the eggplant slices on top of the tomato sauce. Depending on the size of your Dutch oven and the number of slices, you may need to overlap them slightly. Drizzle the reserved sauce over the eggplant slices and sprinkle with the mozzarella and the remaining ¼ cup of Parmigiano-Reggiano.

11. Place the pot in the oven, uncovered, and bake for 12 to 18 minutes, or until the sauce is bubbling and the cheese is melted.

Ratatouille with Navy Beans

ACTIVE TIME
20 MINUTES

TOTAL TIME
1 HOUR

Serves 2

VEGAN

Since the movie *Ratatouille* came out, recipes for the dish have shown up everywhere. At its most complex, ratatouille is made in stages, with all the elements cooked separately, then layered. I've long felt that the fussy process isn't worth the bother, so I simplify. I also add beans to make the dish more substantial. (Please don't call the ratatouille police.)

Kosher salt

1 medium zucchini, sliced ½-inch thick

2 to 3 tablespoons olive oil

½ small onion, sliced (about ⅔ cup)

2 garlic cloves, minced or pressed

½ small green bell pepper, seeded and cut into ½-inch chunks (about ½ cup)

½ small red bell pepper, seeded and cut into ½-inch chunks (about ½ cup)

2 small tomatoes, seeded and diced

1 cup canned navy beans, drained and rinsed

½ teaspoon dried oregano

¼ teaspoon freshly ground black pepper

2 tablespoons minced fresh basil

1. Very liberally salt one side of the zucchini slices. Place the slices salted-side down on a rack placed over a baking sheet. Salt the other side. Let the slices sit for 15 to 20 minutes, or until they start to exude water (you'll see it beading up on the surface of the slices and dripping down into the sheet pan). Rinse the slices and blot them dry. Cut the zucchini slices in half.

2. Place the Dutch oven over medium heat. Add enough oil to coat the bottom of the pot and heat until the oil shimmers. Add the zucchini slices in a single layer and cook without moving for 3 to 5 minutes, or until browned. Turn and brown the other sides, about 3 minutes. Remove to the rack or a plate.

3. Add the onion and garlic to the Dutch oven and season with a pinch of salt. Cook, stirring, until the onions just begin to brown, about 3 minutes.

4. Add the bell peppers and cook for about 3 minutes, or until they just start to brown. Add the zucchini, tomatoes, beans, oregano, and black pepper. Bring to a simmer and cover. Reduce the heat to medium-low and simmer for 15 to 20 minutes, or until the vegetables are soft. If there is too much liquid in the pot, simmer uncovered for a few minutes until it is reduced.

5. Garnish with the basil and serve.

INGREDIENT TIP Most ratatouille recipes call for eggplant. I omit it here because it can be difficult to find an eggplant small enough for a two-serving batch. If you can find a small one, use it instead of the zucchini (or in addition to a small zucchini), salted and rinsed in the same manner as the zucchini.

Oven Risotto with Butternut Squash

According to Dorothy Parker, "eternity is two people and a ham," but the same could be said of butternut squash. Not only is a butternut squash way too big for two people, but it's intimidating as well. When I saw peeled and cut squash at my market, I was sold. Eight ounces might still be too much for one meal, depending on how you're serving it. Roast it all, then use it throughout the week.

1 (8-ounce) container butternut squash, peeled and diced

3 to 4 tablespoons olive oil

Kosher salt

1 large shallot, finely chopped

¾ cup Arborio or Carnaroli rice

¼ cup dry white wine

Pinch dried sage

2½ cups water

1 cup vegetable stock, divided

¼ teaspoon freshly ground black pepper

2 tablespoons unsalted butter

¼ cup grated Parmigiano-Reggiano or similar cheese, plus more for garnish

1. Preheat the oven to 400°F.

2. Add the butternut squash cubes to the Dutch oven and drizzle with enough olive oil to coat the squash completely. Season with salt. Place the pot in the oven, uncovered, and roast the squash for about 15 minutes, then gently stir. Return the pot to the oven for another 15 minutes and stir again. Return to the oven and roast until tender with some crisp edges, probably another 10 to 15 minutes. Remove the squash from the Dutch oven and set aside.

3. Place the Dutch oven over medium heat. Add enough oil to coat the bottom of the pot and heat until the oil shimmers. Add the shallot and cook, stirring, for 3 to 4 minutes, until softened. Add the rice and stir to coat with the oil. Cook for about a minute; move the rice and shallots to the perimeter of the Dutch oven.

4. Add 3 or 4 cubes of the squash to the center of the pot and smash with a potato masher or the back of a spoon until they form a coarse paste. Add the wine and the sage and stir the rice into the squash. Bring to a simmer and cook until the wine is mostly absorbed.

5. While the wine is reducing, mix the water and stock and heat in a saucepan or a heat-proof bowl in the microwave. Pour ½ of the water-stock mixture into the Dutch oven and stir vigorously. Bring to a simmer and cover the Dutch oven.

6. Place the pot in the oven and bake for 15 minutes. Uncover and stir vigorously once more. The rice should be fairly soupy; if it seems at all dry, pour in another ½ cup of the water-stock mixture. Cover the pot and return to the oven. Bake for another 10 to 15 minutes, or until most of the liquid is absorbed and the rice is barely tender.

7. Place the Dutch oven over low heat on the stove top and add ¼ cup of the water-stock mixture. Stir the risotto for 3 to 5 minutes, or until the liquid is mostly absorbed, then stir in the pepper, butter, and half the cheese. Gently stir in as much of the reserved roasted squash as you like and let the risotto sit for a few minutes to warm the squash through.

8. Spoon into bowls and top with the remaining cheese and additional pepper, if desired.

INGREDIENT TIP If your market doesn't sell precut squash in containers, see if you can get the produce manager to cut a butternut in half for you. It will be much easier to peel and dice.

Sofrito and Gruyère–Stuffed Portobello Mushrooms

ACTIVE TIME
20 MINUTES

TOTAL TIME
30 MINUTES
PLUS
MARINATING TIME

Serves 2

My partner and I developed this recipe for a corporate "team building" class several years ago. Our client requested a steak menu but there were a couple of vegetarians in the group. These hearty, savory mushrooms make a wonderful alternative to steak. In fact, they were so good that all the meat lovers wanted them, too.

4 portobello mushrooms, about 3 inches across

4 tablespoons sherry vinegar

4 teaspoons minced fresh oregano or 2 teaspoons dried

4 garlic cloves, minced or pressed, divided

1 teaspoon Dijon mustard

½ teaspoon kosher salt, plus more for seasoning

½ cup extra-virgin olive oil, plus 2 to 3 tablespoons, divided

⅔ cup julienned green bell pepper (about ½ a small pepper)

⅔ cup julienned red, yellow or orange bell pepper (about ½ a small pepper)

1 small onion, sliced thin

¼ teaspoon red pepper flakes

2 ounces Gruyère or Emmenthal cheese (about ½ cup), shredded

1. Prepare the mushrooms by removing the stem and scraping out the gills with a small spoon.

2. In a small bowl, whisk together the vinegar, oregano, half the garlic, mustard, and salt. Slowly whisk in ½ cup of olive oil. Pour the marinade into a sealable plastic bag and add the mushrooms, turning the bag over to coat all the mushrooms. Let them marinate for 1 to 2 hours at room temperature, turning the bag every 15 minutes or so.

3. Preheat the oven to 375°F.

4. While the mushrooms are marinating, place the Dutch oven over medium heat. Add enough of the remaining oil to coat the bottom of the pot and heat until the oil shimmers. Add the bell pepper slices and stir to coat with the oil. Cook without stirring for 2 to 3 minutes, or until the slices just start to brown.

5. Add the onion and remaining garlic, and cook, stirring, until the onion slices start to brown, 2 to 3 minutes. Add the red pepper flakes and salt. Transfer the sofrito mixture to a small bowl.

6. Add another coat of oil to the Dutch oven and let it heat until shimmering. While the oil heats, remove the mushrooms from the marinade and pat dry. Add to the pot, under-side down and cook for 1 to 2 minutes, or until slightly browned. Depending on the size of your Dutch oven, you may need to do this in batches.

7. Turn the mushrooms over, under-side up. Divide the sofrito stuffing evenly among the mushrooms and top with the cheese.

8. Place the mushrooms back in the pot. Place in the oven and bake for 10 minutes or until the cheese has melted and the mushrooms are cooked through.

INGREDIENT TIP If you can find extra-large portobellos, cook two instead of four (you may have leftover sofrito; it's great added to pasta dishes) and use them to make sandwiches on hamburger buns.

Three Cheese–Mushroom Pasta Bake

ACTIVE TIME
15 MINUTES

TOTAL TIME
1 HOUR

Serves 2

Sometimes a recipe I've come across makes an impression on me, but when I go to make it, I can't find it. This was one of those cases. I remembered most of the ingredients and the general procedure, so I just developed my own version. When I found the original recipe (on the *New York Times* cooking website), I discovered that it called for roasted wild mushrooms instead of the creminis I used, but I think my method gets better results with less fuss.

Kosher salt

6 ounces penne, farfalle, or other short pasta

½ pound cremini or white button mushrooms

3 tablespoons extra-virgin olive oil

1 large garlic clove, minced

¾ cup heavy cream

½ cup fresh ricotta

5 ounces fontina cheese, grated (1¼ cups)

¼ teaspoon freshly ground black pepper

2 ounces aged Parmigiano-Reggiano or similar cheese, grated (½ cup)

1. Add 8 cups of water to the Dutch oven and place over high heat. Add about 2 teaspoons kosher salt and bring the water to a boil. Add the pasta and cook according to the package directions. (If you prefer, you can use a separate pot to cook the pasta while you prepare the mushrooms.) Drain, reserving at least a cup of the hot pasta water. Cover the reserved water with a lid or plate to keep warm, and set both the water and the pasta aside.

2. While the water heats and the pasta cooks, wash the mushrooms and trim the stems. Quarter the mushrooms if small to medium; cut into eighths if they are large. Set aside.

3. Preheat the oven to 375°F.

4. When the pasta is done cooking, add the mushrooms to the Dutch oven and cover with enough water to make the mushrooms float. Pour in the oil and season generously with salt. Place the pot over high heat and bring to a boil. Continue boiling until the water has evaporated and you can hear the mushrooms begin to sizzle. Add the garlic and cook, stirring the mushrooms occasionally, until brown on all sides, about 5 minutes.

5. Pour the cream into the Dutch oven. Cook for about 3 minutes, or until the cream has reduced by about one-third.

6. Pour the reserved hot pasta water over the cooked pasta to loosen it up, then add the pasta to the cream and mushrooms in the pot. Stir in the ricotta, fontina, and pepper and toss gently to coat. Sprinkle the Parmigiano-Reggiano cheese over the top of the pasta and place the pot in the oven. Bake for 10 minutes, or until the top is browned and the pasta is bubbling.

INGREDIENT TIP So-called "wild" mushrooms that you find in most markets—shiitakes and oyster mushrooms are the most common—are almost always cultivated these days, but that doesn't mean they aren't good. If you want to try them in this recipe, just substitute them for the cremini or button mushrooms.

Penne Arrabiata

Pasta *all'arrabiata* (which translates as "angry sauce") is loaded with flavor thanks to onions, garlic, and red pepper. It's also a quick and easy weeknight meal. High-quality imported Italian tomatoes can be difficult to find in smaller cans. I find that the addition of a little sun-dried tomato purée deepens and improves the flavor of even ordinary canned tomatoes.

2 teaspoons kosher salt, plus ¼ teaspoon

6 ounces penne

2 to 3 tablespoons extra-virgin olive oil

½ small onion, minced

2 garlic cloves, minced

1 (14-ounce) can diced tomatoes with their juice

1 tablespoon minced or puréed sun-dried tomatoes

½ teaspoon red pepper flakes

2 tablespoons chopped fresh parsley

Grated Parmigiano-Reggiano or similar cheese, to finish

1. Add 8 cups of water to the Dutch oven and place the pot over high heat. Add 2 teaspoons of salt and bring the water to a boil. Add the penne and cook according to the package directions. (If you prefer, you can use a separate pot to cook the pasta while you prepare the sauce.) Drain, reserving at least a cup of the hot pasta water. Cover the water with a lid or plate to keep warm, and set both the water and the pasta aside.

2. Wipe out the inside of the Dutch oven. Place the pot over medium heat and add the olive oil. Heat until the oil shimmers, then add the onion and garlic. Cook, stirring, for 4 to 6 minutes, or until the onion pieces have separated and softened and the garlic is very fragrant. Add the canned tomatoes with their juice, the sun-dried tomatoes, and the red pepper flakes and bring to a simmer. Add the remaining ¼ teaspoon of salt and stir. Bring to a simmer and cook for about 10 minutes.

3. Using a potato masher or the back of a spoon, crush the tomatoes to form a smoother sauce. Taste and adjust the seasoning, adding more red pepper flakes if you want a spicier sauce.

4. Pour the reserved hot pasta water over the cooked penne to loosen it up, then add it to the sauce in the pot. Add the parsley and toss to coat the pasta with the sauce. Sprinkle with the cheese and serve.

TECHNIQUE TIP As with all the pasta dishes in this book, you can save time if you start the water heating before you do anything else. Then prepare the sauce ingredients so they're all ready to go when the pasta is done cooking.

Macaroni and Cheese with Roasted Red Peppers and Caramelized Onions

ACTIVE TIME
35 MINUTES

TOTAL TIME
2 HOURS

Serves 2

The combination of roasted red peppers and caramelized onions with two different kinds of Gouda cheese is sublime. While macaroni and cheese is terrific on its own, these flavors take it to a new level. For the aged Gouda, make sure to look for one aged 18 months or more. The casserole can be served as a stove top version with no topping if you prefer; just skip the first and the last steps.

FOR THE TOPPING

Panko bread crumbs

Butter

Aged Gouda cheese, grated

FOR THE PASTA

2 medium onions, sliced thin (about 2 cups)

2 tablespoons butter, divided

Kosher salt

5 ounces elbow macaroni or small shells

1 tablespoon all-purpose flour

½ teaspoon dried mustard

6 ounces whole milk (¾ cup)

1 ounce cream cheese

6 ounces aged Gouda cheese, shredded (¾ cup)

2 ounces Gouda cheese, shredded (¼ cup)

½ roasted red pepper, diced (about ½ cup)

1. To make the topping, pour out enough panko into the Dutch oven to form a thin, even covering. Measure the panko, then measure out 2 teaspoons of butter and 1 tablespoon of grated aged Gouda for each ½ cup of panko. Melt the butter and stir into the panko, then stir in the cheese. Set aside.

2. To caramelize the onions, place the Dutch oven over medium heat. Add 1 tablespoon of butter and melt over medium heat until it's just starting to foam. Add the onions and stir to coat with the butter. Season with salt and cover the pot. Turn the burner down to low and cook for at least an hour (usually 90 minutes), stirring every 15 minutes or so. The onions will soften, then slowly turn golden and then light amber in color. There should still be a fair amount of liquid in the pot. This process can take longer depending on the moisture level of the onions, but keep the heat low.

3. Uncover and turn the heat up to medium. Cook the onions, stirring occasionally, until they darken to a deep caramel color, the liquid has evaporated, and about ⅓ cup of the onions remains. Transfer to a bowl and set aside.

4. Add 8 cups of water to the Dutch oven and place the pot over high heat. Add 2 teaspoons of salt and bring the water to a boil. Add the macaroni and cook according to the package directions. (If you prefer, you can use a separate pot to cook the pasta while you prepare the sauce.) Drain, reserving at least a cup of the hot pasta water. Cover the water with a lid or plate to keep it warm, and set both the water and the pasta aside.

5. Preheat the oven to 375°F. (This is to finish the mac and cheese with the topping; if you're not using the topping, don't heat the oven.)

6. Return the Dutch oven to medium heat. Add the remaining 1 tablespoon of the butter and melt. When it starts foaming, add the flour and dried mustard. Stir to combine and cook for 2 minutes, or until the mixture turns beige. It should be thick but fairly smooth. Add half the milk and whisk until the mixture is smooth. Add the rest of the milk and whisk again. Let the sauce cook for a minute to thicken up. »

7. Turn the heat to low. Add the cream cheese and stir just until melted. Add the two shredded Gouda cheeses in several stages and stir until each addition is melted. Taste, and add more salt if necessary. Remove the sauce from the heat.

8. Pour the reserved pasta water over the macaroni to loosen it up and stir the drained pasta into the sauce. Stir in the caramelized onions and roasted red pepper. Let the mixture sit for a couple of minutes to warm the vegetables.

9. Spread the macaroni and cheese into an even layer and sprinkle the panko mixture over. Place the pot in the preheated oven and bake for about 10 minutes, or until the topping is browned and the mixture is bubbling.

INGREDIENT TIP If you want plain macaroni and cheese, omit the onions and the red peppers. Substitute aged Cheddar for the aged Gouda, and Monterey Jack cheese for the regular Gouda.

Vegetable Korma

ACTIVE TIME
30 MINUTES

TOTAL TIME
30 MINUTES

Serves 2

Back in my single days in San Francisco, there was a great Indian restaurant that delivered. I ordered from them more times than I care to admit, and one of my favorite dishes was a very spicy vegetable korma. This is my version of that dish, with toned down spice level. If you prefer to use fresh vegetables instead of frozen, steam about 2 cups of veggies until crisp-tender.

⅔ cup canned diced tomatoes, drained (about half a 14-ounce can)

½ small onion, cut into chunks

1 small jalapeño pepper, seeded and cut into chunks

1 teaspoon grated fresh ginger

2 medium garlic cloves, smashed

1 teaspoon ground coriander

½ teaspoon ground cardamom

½ teaspoon ground cinnamon

¼ teaspoon ground turmeric

1 teaspoon kosher salt

¼ teaspoon freshly ground black pepper

2 to 3 tablespoons vegetable oil

2 cups mixed frozen "stir-fry" vegetables, thawed

½ cup frozen peas, thawed

¼ teaspoon red pepper flakes (optional)

¼ cup whole-milk yogurt

1. Place the tomatoes, onion, jalapeño, ginger, garlic, coriander, cardamom, cinnamon, turmeric, salt, and pepper in a blender or small food processor and blend to a smooth paste (or use an immersion blender and a deep sturdy cup to blend).

2. Place the Dutch oven over medium heat. Add enough oil to coat the bottom of the pot and heat until the oil shimmers. Add the puréed tomato mixture and bring to a simmer. Cook for about 15 minutes, or until the sauce has thickened slightly and is very fragrant.

3. Add the thawed mixed vegetables and peas and bring back to a simmer. Cook for about 5 minutes, or until the vegetables are heated through. Taste and add the red pepper flakes if you want a spicier sauce. Stir in the yogurt and bring back to just a simmer. Serve over steamed basmati rice or with Garlic Naan (page 188).

Spiced Lentils and Rice with Kale

ACTIVE TIME
15 MINUTES

TOTAL TIME
40 MINUTES

Serves 2

VEGAN

This recipe combines lentils with earthy spices and adds greens for an easy one-pot meatless meal. Dried lentils have an advantage over other beans and legumes, because they don't require long soaking and are relatively quick to cook. They cook at about the same rate as rice, which may be why the combination is so common.

½ cup brown lentils

2 to 3 tablespoons olive oil

½ medium onion, chopped

2 garlic cloves, minced

Kosher salt

⅓ cup long-grain rice

1 teaspoon ground cumin

½ teaspoon ground coriander

¼ teaspoon cayenne pepper

⅛ teaspoon ground cinnamon

3 cups low-sodium vegetable stock

2 cups chopped kale or other study greens

2 tablespoons chopped toasted pistachios

1. Rinse the lentils and then place them in a small bowl. Cover with water and let them soak while you chop and cook the onion and garlic.

2. Place the Dutch oven over medium-high heat. Add enough oil to coat the bottom of the pot and heat until the oil shimmers. Add the onion and cook, stirring, for 6 to 8 minutes, or until browned. Add the garlic and season with salt. Cook for a minute or so, or until the garlic is fragrant.

3. Add the rice and stir to coat with the oil. Cook, stirring, for 2 to 3 minutes, or until the rice smells nutty. Add the cumin, coriander, cayenne, and cinnamon and stir to coat the rice with the spices.

4. Cook for a minute, then add the stock and ¼ teaspoon of salt.

5. Drain the lentils and add to the Dutch oven. Stir to combine. Bring the liquid to a simmer and stir again. Cover and reduce the heat to low. After cooking for 15 minutes, stir gently. Taste the rice and lentils; they should be a bit firm in the center but almost done. Add the kale and press into the rice and lentil mixture. Cover and cook for an additional 8 to 10 minutes, or until the kale, rice, and lentils are all tender.

6. Ladle into bowls and top with the pistachios.

INGREDIENT TIP Pistachios are common in Middle Eastern dishes, and they add a welcome crunch to this dish. To save time, look for dry roasted pistachios out of the shells, either salted or unsalted. As with all nuts, freeze any extra. Nut oils go rancid quickly and freezing is the best way to keep them fresh.

Masoor Dal

ACTIVE TIME
25 MINUTES

TOTAL TIME
1 HOUR

Serves 2

VEGAN

The word *dal* (or *daal*) technically refers to lentils, with *masoor dal* meaning the split red lentils that are used here. But the term is also used to refer to the finished dish, which is traditionally cooked with spices and chiles, with a topping of browned onions and garlic. I first tried the dish when I was assisting an Indian chef instructor at a cooking class. His version was more time consuming, so I've simplified it but kept the spirit of his recipe.

1 medium onion

4 garlic cloves

2 to 4 tablespoons vegetable oil

1 jalapeño pepper or serrano chile, seeded and diced

1 cup dried red lentils, rinsed

3½ cups water

½ teaspoon ground turmeric

¼ teaspoon ground cumin

1 bay leaf

1 teaspoon kosher salt

1 cup canned diced tomatoes, drained

2 tablespoons coarsely chopped fresh cilantro

1. Slice half the onion, and dice the other half. Slice two cloves of garlic and mince or press the other two. Set aside the diced onion and the minced garlic.

2. Place the Dutch oven over medium heat. Add enough oil to coat the bottom of the pot and heat until the oil shimmers. Add the sliced onion and garlic. Stir to coat the onion and garlic slices with the oil, then let them sit in a single layer until browned, about 4 minutes. Don't stir until you can see them browning. Stir them to expose the other side to the heat and repeat. The onion and garlic should be browned, but still slightly firm. Remove the mixture from the pan and set aside.

3. Add more oil if necessary to coat the bottom of the Dutch oven. When it's hot, add the chopped onions, minced garlic, and jalapeño; cook, stirring, for 2 minutes, or until softened slightly and fragrant. Add the lentils, water, turmeric, cumin, bay leaf, and salt, and bring to a simmer. Cover and cook for 15 minutes, stirring once or twice.

4. Add the tomatoes. Simmer, uncovered, for another 5 to 8 minutes, or until the lentils are tender.

5. When the lentils are done, stir in the reserved onion-garlic mixture and simmer for another minute or two, or until the onions are warmed through. Garnish with the cilantro and serve plain or over rice.

Spicy Garlic Tofu with Cashews and Spinach

ACTIVE TIME
30 MINUTES

TOTAL TIME
30 MINUTES

Serves 2

VEGAN

Not everyone loves tofu, but deep-fried in spicy sauce it's irresistible. Fresh spinach and cashews add a nutritional boost to this otherwise indulgent dish.

FOR THE TOFU

½ pound extra-firm tofu

Vegetable oil for frying

5 to 6 ounces fresh baby spinach

½ cup cornstarch

1 tablespoon minced garlic (about 3 cloves)

2 teaspoons minced ginger

3 scallions, minced

¼ cup roasted unsalted cashews

FOR THE SAUCE

1 tablespoon soy sauce

2 tablespoons rice vinegar

¼ cup water or vegetable stock

2 teaspoons Asian chile-garlic sauce, like Sriracha (or more)

¼ teaspoon freshly ground black pepper

1 teaspoon cornstarch

1 teaspoon granulated sugar

2 teaspoons sesame oil

1. Slice the tofu into ½-inch-thick slices. Place on a layer of paper towels and cover with another layer. Press lightly to dry the slices. Uncover and let air-dry for 15 minutes while you prepare the sauce and aromatics, and cook the spinach.

2. For the sauce, whisk all the ingredients together in a small bowl. Keep the whisk handy, as you'll need to whisk the sauce again right before using.

3. Place the Dutch oven over medium heat. Add enough oil to coat the bottom of the pot and heat until the oil shimmers. Add the spinach and toss just to wilt. Remove from the Dutch oven and wipe the pot dry.

4. To make the tofu, increase the heat to high, and pour in enough oil to form a layer about 1-inch deep. Heat to 365°F. While the oil is heating, cut the tofu slices into bite-size pieces, about 1 inch by 1½ inches. Pour the cornstarch into a small bowl and toss the tofu pieces in the cornstarch until they are coated heavily.

5. Use a slotted spoon or spider to remove about half the tofu from the cornstarch and add to the hot oil. Cook for 4 to 5 minutes or until golden brown and crisp. Use the spoon or spider to remove the pieces to a rack placed over a sheet pan, and let the oil heat back up to 365°F. Repeat with the remaining tofu. (Depending on the size of your Dutch oven, you may have to cook three batches; don't crowd the pan).

6. Pour off all but a light coating of the oil. Return the pot to medium-high heat and add the garlic, ginger, and scallions. Cook, stirring, for a minute or two, or until fragrant and just slightly browned. Whisk the sauce to combine, and add to the Dutch oven. Bring to a simmer and let cook for 2 to 3 minutes, or until thickened. Add the tofu, spinach, and cashews, and toss gently to coat with the sauce. Serve with or without steamed rice.

TECHNIQUE TIP For extra-crisp tofu, use the batter and frying technique from the Baja Fish Tacos (page 96) rather than dredging the tofu in cornstarch.

FISH & SHELLFISH

chapter five

Baja Fish Tacos with Avocado Cream

This recipe not only serves two, but is perfect for making together. One person can focus on the fish, and the other can make the slaw and avocado cream. If you're the sole cook, you can make the avocado cream ahead of time; it will keep about a day in the fridge. The coleslaw will keep for several hours as well, so the only last-minute task is the fish.

FOR THE TACOS

4 to 6 corn or flour tortillas

8 to 10 ounces firm white fish such as cod or tilapia

Kosher salt

White rice flour for dusting fish, plus ½ cup

Vegetable oil for frying

½ cup all-purpose flour

½ teaspoon baking powder

¼ teaspoon fine salt

½ cup vodka

½ cup club soda

FOR THE SLAW

1 cup shredded red or white cabbage

½ teaspoon kosher salt

1 scallion, minced

1 small jalapeño pepper, seeded and minced

1 tablespoon coarsely chopped fresh cilantro

Juice of ½ lime (about 1 tablespoon)

FOR THE AVOCADO CREAM

½ medium ripe Hass avocado, peeled and cut into chunks

¼ cup sour cream

¼ cup loosely packed fresh cilantro leaves

2 tablespoons medium green salsa (store-bought or homemade)

Juice of ½ lime (about 1 tablespoon)

¼ teaspoon kosher salt

⅛ teaspoon ground cumin

1. Preheat the oven to 200°F. Wrap the tortillas in aluminum foil and place in the oven to warm.

2. Cut the fish into pieces about 3 inches by 1 inch and season with kosher salt. Dust lightly on both sides with rice flour.

3. Place the Dutch oven over medium heat. Add about 2 inches of oil and heat until the oil registers 365°F to 375°F. While the oil heats, whisk together ½ cup of rice flour, the all-purpose flour, baking powder, and fine salt in a medium bowl. Stir in the vodka and club soda to the dry ingredients to make a medium-thick batter.

4. Place a rack over a sheet pan and place it in the oven.

5. Use tongs to place one-third to one-half of the fish pieces in the batter. Flip and stir as needed to cover with batter. One at a time, place the fish pieces into the oil. Don't crowd the Dutch oven; it's best to cook at least two batches. Fry about 3 to 4 minutes, or until golden brown. If the oil is not deep enough to cover the fish pieces, turn them halfway through. Move the cooked fish to the sheet pan in the oven to keep warm while you finish cooking the rest of the fish.

6. For the slaw, place the cabbage in a small colander or the basket of a salad spinner. Season with the salt and let sit for 15 minutes. Rinse well and pat (or spin) dry. Add the scallion, jalapeño, and cilantro and toss gently. Sprinkle with the lime juice and toss again.

7. For the avocado cream, place all the ingredients in a small food processor and pulse until smooth. If you don't have a small food processor, mince the cilantro. Put the avocado in a small bowl and use a potato masher or large fork to mash it. Add the rest of the ingredients and stir to combine. Don't worry if it's not completely smooth.

8. To serve, place 2 or 3 pieces of fish on a tortilla and add a spoonful of slaw, then drizzle with the avocado cream.

PERFECT PAIR This casual meal pairs perfectly with a classic margarita. For two cocktails, pour 4 ounces of 100% blue agave tequila, 2 ounces triple sec, and 2 ounces fresh lime juice into a cocktail shaker. Fill with ice and shake until the drink is thoroughly chilled. Pour into two chilled cocktail glasses, or over ice in rocks glasses if you prefer.

Teriyaki Salmon with Braised Bok Choy

ACTIVE TIME
20 MINUTES

TOTAL TIME
35 MINUTES
PLUS 30 MINUTES
MARINATING TIME

Serves 2

If your only experience with teriyaki sauce is the overly sweet bottled stuff, making your own can be an epiphany. While the honey does add sweetness, it's balanced by rice vinegar and soy sauce. The sauce does double duty here as a marinade and cooking sauce (triple duty if you use the rest as a glaze as outlined in the tip following the recipe). You'll never go back to the bottle.

½ cup soy sauce

3 tablespoons honey

1 tablespoon rice vinegar

1 tablespoon rice wine or dry sherry

2 teaspoons minced fresh ginger

2 garlic cloves, smashed

2 (6- to 8-ounce) ounce salmon fillets, skin removed

1 to 2 tablespoons vegetable oil

1 teaspoon sesame oil

3 heads baby bok choy, root ends trimmed off and cut in half through the root

1 tablespoon toasted sesame seeds

1. In a small bowl, whisk together the soy sauce, honey, rice vinegar, rice wine, ginger, and garlic, making sure that the honey is dissolved. Set aside ¼ cup of the mixture and pour the rest into a sealable plastic bag. Put the salmon fillets in the bag and seal, squeezing as much air out as possible. Let the salmon marinate for 30 minutes or so, turning the bag every 10 minutes.

2. Preheat the oven to 375°F.

3. While the salmon marinates, place the Dutch oven over medium heat. Add enough vegetable oil to coat the bottom of the pot and heat until it shimmers. Add the sesame oil and the bok choy, cut-side down. Cook for a minute or two, or until the bok choy just starts to brown a little. Turn the bok choy and cook for another minute. Whisk the reserved ¼ cup of sauce with 2 tablespoons of water, and pour it over the bok choy.

4. Remove the salmon fillets from the bag and place on top of the bok choy. Place the Dutch oven, uncovered, in the oven and bake the salmon and bok choy for 15 to 20 minutes, or until done to your liking.

TECHNIQUE TIP For extra flavor, after removing the salmon from the marinade, pour the marinade into a small saucepan. While the salmon cooks, bring the marinade to a boil over medium-high heat and simmer to reduce to a thick syrup. Before serving the salmon, brush the top of the salmon with the glaze.

Salmon with Roasted Fennel, Garlic, and Tomatoes

ACTIVE TIME
15 MINUTES

TOTAL TIME
1 HOUR

Serves 2

The mild licorice flavor of fennel goes especially well with fish, and this pairing with salmon and tomatoes is a classic. Roasting the salmon under the vegetables keeps it moist and perfectly cooked. While tradition may dictate white wine with fish, the stronger flavors in this dish marry well with a dry rosé or even light red wine. Wines from (or styled after) the Rhône area of France are a good choice.

½ small fennel bulb

1 cup cherry or grape tomatoes, halved

6 garlic cloves, peeled and quartered

2 tablespoons olive oil

Kosher salt

2 (6-ounce) salmon fillets, skin on or off

Freshly ground black pepper

1. Preheat the oven to 375°F.

2. Trim the root and any stems or fronds off the fennel. Cut out the core from the bottom center of the bulb, and cut into pieces about ¼-inch thick. Add the fennel slices, tomatoes, and garlic to the Dutch oven and drizzle the olive oil over the vegetables. Season with salt and toss gently to coat.

3. Roast the vegetables, uncovered, for about 10 minutes. Remove the pot from the oven and toss the vegetables. Roast for another 5 to 10 minutes, or until the fennel and garlic begin to soften and brown in spots.

4. While the vegetables are cooking, season both sides of the salmon with salt and pepper.

5. When the vegetables are done roasting, remove the pot from the oven. Move the vegetables to the perimeter of the Dutch oven and place the salmon fillets on the bottom of the pot. Spoon the vegetables over the salmon.

6. Return the pot to the oven and roast for another 15 minutes, or until the salmon flakes apart but is still very moist.

Penne with Smoked Trout and Corn

ACTIVE TIME
30 MINUTES

TOTAL TIME
30 MINUTES

Serves 2

Years ago, my then-boyfriend got a "beer cuisine" cookbook for his birthday. While the boyfriend and book are long gone, the memories of the smoked trout and corn remain. Many years later, I found a copy of the book, but by then, I'd come up with my own version of the recipe, which is at least as good as the original, if not better.

2 teaspoons kosher salt

5 to 6 ounces penne

2 tablespoons butter

⅔ cup blanched fresh corn kernels or frozen corn, thawed

2 scallions, chopped

¼ cup dry white wine

⅔ cup heavy cream

½ teaspoon prepared horseradish

½ teaspoon grated lemon zest

¼ teaspoon freshly ground white pepper

4 to 5 ounces hot-smoked trout, flaked (about half a medium trout)

1½ tablespoons minced chives, for garnish

1. Add 8 cups of water to the Dutch oven and place the pot over high heat. Add the salt and bring the water to a boil. Add the pasta and cook according to the package directions. (If you prefer, you can use a separate pot to cook the pasta while you prepare the sauce.) Drain, reserving at least 1 cup of the hot pasta water. Cover the water with a lid or plate to keep warm, and set both the water and the pasta aside.

2. Wipe the Dutch oven dry. Place it over medium heat and add the butter. When the butter stops foaming, add the corn and scallions and cook, stirring, for about 3 minutes, or until the scallions soften slightly.

3. Turn the heat up to medium-high and add the white wine. Bring the wine to a boil and reduce until it's almost all evaporated. Add the cream and bring to a boil. Cook until it's reduced by about one-third and turn the heat off. Stir in the horseradish, lemon zest, and white pepper.

4. Pour the reserved hot pasta water over the cooked pasta to loosen it up, then add it to the sauce along with the smoked trout. Toss gently and divide it into two pasta bowls. Garnish with the minced chives, if desired.

INGREDIENT TIP If you don't have chives for a garnish, reserve a couple of teaspoons of the scallion greens to top the finished dish. The bright mild onion flavor is a wonderful complement for the other ingredients.

Tilapia Puttanesca

ACTIVE TIME
15 MINUTES

TOTAL TIME
1 HOUR
10 MINUTES

Serves 2

I came up with this recipe when I was making the Mexican dish Snapper Vera Cruz, which is fish baked under a spicy tomato sauce. Why not try an Italian version? While the sauce takes some time to simmer, the hands-on work is pretty fast and easy.

2 to 3 tablespoons extra-virgin olive oil

2 garlic cloves, minced

1 small shallot, minced

1 teaspoon anchovy paste

½ teaspoon red pepper flakes

1 (14-ounce) can diced tomatoes, with their juice

2 tablespoons pitted Kalamata olives

2 teaspoons drained capers

2 tablespoons minced fresh basil, divided

2 (6- to 8-ounce) tilapia fillets (or other firm white fish)

Kosher salt

1. Preheat the oven to 350°F.

2. Place the Dutch oven over medium heat. Add enough oil to heavily coat the bottom of the pot and heat until the oil shimmers. Add the garlic and shallot and cook, stirring, for about 3 minutes, or until the vegetables are soft and light brown in spots.

3. Stir in the anchovy paste and red pepper flakes and cook for a minute. Add the tomatoes with their juice and bring to a simmer. Cover and cook for 15 to 20 minutes. Use the back of a fork or a potato masher to crush the tomatoes slightly.

4. Add the olives, capers, and half the basil and return to a simmer. Cook, uncovered, for 10 minutes. Taste and adjust the seasoning only if necessary, as the anchovies, olives, and capers add plenty of salt to the dish.

5. Sprinkle the fish fillets with salt. Place them in the Dutch oven and spoon most of the sauce over them, so that they're covered. Place the pot, uncovered, in the oven and bake for 10 to 12 minutes, or until the fish flakes with a fork. Sprinkle with the remaining basil.

Mussel and Potato Chowder

Most recipes for mussel chowder call for removing the mussels from their shell. While this is undoubtedly less messy, I prefer to leave the mussels in the shell. That way, the dish becomes two courses: first, you get to dip the mussels in the soup and eat them as a first course, and then you have a delicious fennel and potato soup to eat afterwards, with (sometimes) the bonus of a stray mussel or two.

ACTIVE TIME
20 MINUTES

TOTAL TIME
30 MINUTES

Serves 2

½ medium fennel bulb
(or 1 small bulb)

3 tablespoons butter, divided

1 large shallot, sliced

3 garlic cloves, sliced

¼ cup white wine

2¾ cups whole milk

½ teaspoon kosher salt

2 medium Yukon Gold potatoes, peeled and cut into ½-inch cubes

1 pound mussels, scrubbed and beards removed

1 teaspoon lemon zest

1 tablespoon chopped fresh parsley

1. Trim the root and any stems or fronds off the fennel. Cut out the core from the bottom center of the bulb, and cut into pieces about ¼-inch thick, then cut each piece into 2 to 3 pieces.

2. Place the Dutch oven over medium heat and add 2 tablespoons of butter. When it has just stopped foaming, add the fennel, shallot, and garlic. Cook, stirring, for 4 to 5 minutes, until soft and fragrant.

3. Pour in the wine and bring to a boil, reducing by about half. Add the milk, salt, and potatoes and bring to a simmer. Cook, uncovered, for 15 minutes or until the potatoes are tender.

4. Turn the heat to medium-high and bring the soup to a boil. Add the mussels and cover the Dutch oven. Cook for 3 minutes, then stir the mussels. Cover again and cook for 2 minutes, or until all the mussel shells have opened (discard any that have not opened). Stir in the remaining 1 tablespoon of butter, the lemon zest, and parsley. Serve immediately.

Linguine with Clams

I can't think about linguine with clams without thinking about Mike Damone's dating advice in the movie *Fast Times at Ridgemont High*: "When ordering food, you find out what she wants, then order for the both of you. It's a classy move. 'Now, the lady will have the linguini and white clam sauce, and a Coke with no ice.'" While Coke may not be the best pairing, the dish is a winner.

3 tablespoons butter, divided

2 large garlic cloves, minced

½ cup dry white wine

1 tablespoon freshly squeezed lemon juice

¼ teaspoon red pepper flakes

2 pounds small clams, (such as littleneck) well scrubbed

2 teaspoons kosher salt

6 ounces linguine

2 tablespoons heavy cream

2 tablespoons chopped fresh parsley

1. Place the Dutch oven over medium heat. Add 1 tablespoon of butter. When the butter stops foaming, add the garlic and cook, stirring, for 1 minute or until the garlic is fragrant.

2. Add the wine, lemon juice, red pepper flakes, and 1 cup of water. Turn the heat up and bring the liquid to a boil. Add the clams and cover the pot. Cook for 6 to 8 minutes, or until the clams have opened. Pour the clams and liquid into a large bowl to cool, discarding any clams that have not opened.

3. Add 8 cups of water to the Dutch oven and place the pot over high heat. Add the salt and bring the water to a boil. Add the pasta and cook according to the package directions. Drain, reserving at least 1 cup of the hot pasta water.

4. While preparing the pasta, remove the clams from the shells and set aside in a small bowl. Let the liquid settle in the large bowl.

5. When the pasta is done and draining, carefully pour the clam liquid into the now-empty Dutch oven, leaving the last couple of tablespoons behind so you don't get any grit in the sauce. Place the pot over medium heat and bring the liquid to a boil, reducing it by about one-third. Stir in the remaining 2 tablespoons of butter and the cream and bring back to a boil.

6. Pour the reserved pasta water over the linguine to loosen it up and add the pasta to the Dutch oven. Toss to coat the pasta with the sauce. Turn the heat off and add the shelled clams and parsley and toss to combine and heat the clams.

7. Ladle into bowls and serve immediately.

TECHNIQUE TIP While many recipes call for much more water for cooking pasta, you really don't need it. The smaller amount called for here is plenty for two servings of pasta, and it will come to a boil much faster than a giant pot of water, especially if you cover the pot while it's heating. Just be sure to stir the pasta occasionally so it doesn't stick.

Thai Shrimp and Vegetable Curry

ACTIVE TIME
25 MINUTES

TOTAL TIME
25 MINUTES

Serves 2

With a can of coconut milk and a good store-bought Thai curry paste, this dish comes together quickly, but tastes like you spent all afternoon making it. I use the Mae Ploy brand of curry paste; if you can't find it, you may need to adjust the seasoning with additional lime juice, sugar, or fish sauce. The final dish, like many Thai dishes, should have a good balance of salty, sweet, and sour. Serve with a light (not "lite") lager. Singha is probably the brand of Thai beer that's best known in the United States, but any mild beer without lots of hops will pair well.

1 (14-ounce) can full-fat coconut milk

Vegetable or coconut oil (optional)

1 tablespoon Thai red curry paste (or more for seasoning)

1 teaspoon freshly squeezed lime juice (optional)

1 teaspoon sugar (optional)

1 small zucchini, cut into ¼-inch rounds

½ small onion, sliced thin

½ small red bell pepper, seeded and cut into bite-size pieces

8 to 10 ounces medium shrimp, peeled and deveined

1 (5-ounce) bag baby spinach

2 tablespoons chopped fresh basil

2 tablespoons coarsely chopped roasted salted cashews

1. Open the can of coconut milk without shaking it. Depending on the brand, you should see a thick layer of almost solid coconut "cream" on the top of the can. If so, scoop out 2 to 3 tablespoons of it and add to the Dutch oven. If not, add enough vegetable or coconut oil to the Dutch oven to form a thick coat on the bottom. Place the pot over medium heat to melt the coconut fat or heat the oil until it shimmers.

2. Add the curry paste and smash it down into the oil to fry it slightly, about 2 minutes. Add the rest of the can of coconut milk and stir to dissolve. Bring to a simmer and taste. Thai curries should have a balance of hot, sour, and sweet flavors, so add more paste, the optional lime juice, or sugar as necessary.

3. Add the zucchini, onion, and bell pepper and simmer for 10 minutes, or until the vegetables are just tender.

4. Add the shrimp and spinach and bring back to a simmer. Cook for 5 minutes, or until the shrimp are cooked through. Serve over rice (if desired), garnished with the basil and cashews.

Fettuccine with Shrimp and Tomato Cream Sauce

ACTIVE TIME
30 MINUTES

TOTAL TIME
30 MINUTES

Serves 2

Inspired by a recipe by Biba Caggiano from her book *Trattoria*, this is one of the first recipes I specifically developed for two. I've been making it for 10 years, and plan to keep making it for many more. The cream and brandy mellow the tang of the red pepper flakes and tomatoes. It's as easy a dish to eat as it is to make.

2 teaspoons kosher salt, plus more for seasoning

5 to 6 ounces of fettuccine or linguine

2 to 3 tablespoons olive oil

8 ounces raw shrimp, peeled and deveined

1 large garlic clove, minced

⅓ cup brandy

1 cup strained tomatoes (or tomato sauce)

¼ teaspoon red pepper flakes

1 to 2 tablespoons cream

2 teaspoons minced fresh basil for garnish (optional)

1. Add 8 cups of water to the Dutch oven and place the pot over high heat. Add 2 teaspoons of salt and bring the water to a boil. Add the pasta and cook according to the package directions. (If you prefer, you can use a separate pot to cook the pasta while you prepare the sauce.) Drain, reserving at least 1 cup of the hot pasta water. Cover the water with a lid or plate to keep warm, and set both the water and the pasta aside.

2. Wipe the Dutch oven dry. Place it over medium-high heat and add enough oil to coat the bottom of the pot. Heat until the oil shimmers and flows like water. Add the shrimp and cook, stirring, just until the shrimp curl up and turn opaque, about 2 minutes. Use a slotted spoon or spatula to transfer the shrimp to a small bowl.

3. Add the garlic and cook, stirring, until the garlic is fragrant and barely golden.

4. Turn the heat off and add the brandy, being careful to keep your face away from the pot (in case the vapor ignites). Turn the heat back on to medium-high and bring the brandy to a boil. Cook until the brandy is mostly evaporated, 3 to 6 minutes.

5. Add the strained tomatoes, red pepper flakes, and a big pinch of salt and simmer. Cook for 2 to 3 minutes and then stir in the cream. Taste and adjust the seasoning.

6. Pour the reserved hot pasta water over the cooked pasta to loosen it up, then add it to the sauce along with the shrimp. Toss gently and divide it into two pasta bowls. Garnish with the minced basil (if using).

TECHNIQUE TIP If you use the Dutch oven to cook the pasta, take advantage of the time when the water is heating and pasta is cooking to prepare the other ingredients (peeling the shrimp, mincing the garlic, etc.).

POULTRY

chapter six

Mexican Green Rice–Stuffed Cornish Hen

ACTIVE TIME
25 MINUTES

TOTAL TIME
1 HOUR
10 MINUTES

Serves 2

Everyone loves roast chicken but that can be tricky when cooking for two. A Cornish hen, also called a Rock Cornish hen or Cornish game hen, weighing between one and two pounds, is the perfect bird for two, especially when stuffed with chile-seasoned rice.

1 small poblano chile, seeded and cut into 3 or 4 fairly flat pieces

½ small jalapeño pepper, seeded

1 to 2 tablespoons olive oil

½ very small onion, chopped (about ¼ cup)

½ cup long-grain white rice

1 cup low-sodium chicken stock or water

1 teaspoon kosher salt, divided

¼ teaspoon chili powder

¼ teaspoon paprika

¼ teaspoon granulated garlic or onion

1 large Cornish hen (1¾ to 2 pounds)

¼ cup minced fresh cilantro

1. Set the broiler on high, with the rack in the highest position. Place the poblano and jalapeño, skin-side up, on a broiler pan or baking sheet and broil until they're blackened and their skins puff. Place in a bowl and cover for 10 to 15 minutes. Peel the skin off and chop the chiles.

2. Preheat the oven to 350°F.

3. Place the Dutch oven over medium heat. Add enough oil to coat the bottom of the pot and heat until the oil shimmers. Add the onion and cook, stirring, for 4 to 5 minutes, or until the onion pieces have separated and have softened. Add the rice and stir to coat with the oil. Cook for about 1 minute. Stir in the chopped chiles.

4. Add the chicken stock and ½ teaspoon of salt and stir to combine. Bring the liquid to a strong simmer and cover the pot. Place it in the oven and cook for 18 minutes.

5. While the rice is cooking, mix together the remaining ½ teaspoon of salt, the chili powder, paprika, and granulated garlic. Sprinkle it over the Cornish hen on all sides.

6. When the rice is done cooking, remove it from the oven and let it sit, covered, for 15 minutes. Gently fluff the rice and mix in the cilantro. Remove the rice from the Dutch oven and wash the pot.

7. Turn the oven up to 375°F. Brush the bottom of the Dutch oven with oil and place it in the oven, uncovered, to heat.

8. Spoon the rice into the cavity of the Cornish hen, packing it firmly. Depending on the size of the hen, you'll probably have rice left over. You can rewarm it to serve with the hen, or refrigerate it for another meal.

9. If you have a rack that will fit in the bottom of the Dutch oven, place it inside and put the hen on it. If not, place the hen directly on the bottom of the pot.

10. Roast the hen, uncovered, for 30 to 40 minutes, or until the thigh meat registers 165°F on a meat thermometer. (If you don't have a meat thermometer, cut into one of the thighs. The juices should run clear.)

11. Spoon the rice out of the hen onto two plates. Cut the leg-thigh quarters from the hen and carve the breast meat off the bones to serve.

TECHNIQUE TIP A cake cooling rack is ideal for roasting the hen in this recipe. They're round, and come in several different sizes, so you can probably find one that fits in your pot.

Crisp Braised Cornish Hen with Lemon and Garlic

ACTIVE TIME
20 MINUTES

TOTAL TIME
2 HOURS

Serves 2

This dish was inspired by a rather complicated recipe that I came across for a roasted chicken Provençal. I loved the flavors, but knew that I'd have to scale down the difficulty level if I (or anyone else) stood a chance of making it with any frequency. Be forewarned that the preparation of the bird is a bit involved. To cut down on prep work and time, use chicken thighs instead of a whole Cornish hen, and increase the baking time to 40 to 45 minutes.

1 medium Cornish hen (1½ to 2 pounds)

Kosher salt

⅓ cup all-purpose flour

2 to 3 tablespoons olive oil

⅓ cup dry white wine

¼ cup low-sodium chicken stock (or more)

½ teaspoon dried thyme (or 1 teaspoon fresh)

1 small lemon, cut into 8 wedges

8 to 10 garlic cloves, peeled but left whole

1. Place the hen on a cutting board with the back up. Find the fleshy little extension at the base of the spine and position the bird so that is nearest to you. With a sturdy pair of scissors, start at one side of that fleshy piece and cut up along the side of the backbone until you've reached the other side. Then do the same with the other side of the backbone. Flip the bird over and press your hand down over the breast, pushing hard enough to crack the breastbone and flatten the bird. Cut the leg-thigh quarters off, and cut through or along the breastbone and cartilage to cut the breast in half. Leave the wings attached to the breast pieces.

2. Preheat the oven to 375°F.

3. Salt the quarters of the hen on both sides. Place the flour in a shallow bowl and dredge the quarters to coat lightly with flour.

4. Place the Dutch oven over medium heat. Add enough oil to coat the bottom of the pot and heat until the oil shimmers. Place the hen pieces in the pot skin-side down and cook without moving until the pieces are lightly browned, about 4 minutes. If not all the pieces of chicken fit comfortably, brown in batches. Turn and brown the other side. Remove the pieces from the Dutch oven. Pour off any accumulated fat from the Dutch oven.

5. Pour in the white wine and chicken stock and stir in the thyme. Place the Cornish hen pieces back in the pot. The liquid should come about halfway up the hen pieces; add more stock if necessary. Nestle the lemon wedges and garlic cloves among the pieces.

6. Bake, uncovered, for 25 to 35 minutes, or until the meat is cooked through and the skin is browned and crisp. Check the pot about halfway through the cooking and add more stock if the Dutch oven is too dry.

7. To serve, remove the Cornish hen pieces and divide them between two plates. Serve with the sauce, including the garlic cloves and lemon pieces.

Chicken and Herb Dumplings

ACTIVE TIME
45 MINUTES

TOTAL TIME
1 HOUR
15 MINUTES

Serves 2

One of my favorite dinners growing up was chicken and dumplings. Mom didn't make it too often because it was time consuming. Its rarity made it even more appealing. For years, her version was my standard, but I've recently made some changes, and—sorry, Mom!—mine is better. But I still use her dumpling recipe and method; there's no improving on them.

FOR THE HERBED CHICKEN

2 to 3 skinless boneless chicken thighs (8 to 10 ounces total)

Kosher salt

3 to 4 tablespoons vegetable oil

¼ cup all-purpose flour

¼ teaspoon freshly ground black pepper

3½ cups chicken stock

1 thyme sprig (or ¼ teaspoon dried)

1 oregano sprig (or ¼ teaspoon dried)

1 medium carrot, peeled and cut into ¼-inch-thick coins

1 celery stalk, cut into slices about ¼-inch thick

½ cup pearl onions

⅓ cup frozen peas, thawed

FOR THE DUMPLINGS

⅔ cup all-purpose flour

1¼ teaspoons baking powder

½ teaspoon kosher salt

⅛ teaspoon dried thyme

⅛ teaspoon dried oregano

1 tablespoon melted butter

1 egg yolk

¼ cup whole milk

1. Season the chicken thighs on both sides with salt and set aside while you make the dumpling dough.

2. For the dumplings, in a medium bowl, whisk together the flour, baking powder, salt, thyme, and oregano. In a small bowl, whisk together the melted butter, egg yolk, and milk and add to the dry ingredients. Stir with a large fork (the whisk will get clogged) just until the dough holds together. It should be sticky; if it's too dry, add another teaspoon or two of milk. Cover with plastic wrap and refrigerate.

3. Place the Dutch oven over medium heat. Add enough oil to form a layer about ⅛-inch thick and heat until the oil shimmers.

4. While the oil is heating, prepare the chicken. In a shallow bowl, mix the flour with ¼ teaspoon salt and pepper. Dredge the chicken thighs in the flour mixture, turning to coat both sides. Reserve the extra flour.

5. When the oil is hot, add the chicken thighs. Cook for 5 to 6 minutes, or until the thighs are golden brown. Turn and cook for another 5 minutes or so, until the second side is browned.

6. Pour off all but about 2 tablespoons of the oil. Still over medium heat, add 2 tablespoons of the reserved flour mixture and stir to combine. Cook for 5 minutes, stirring constantly, or until the roux mixture is golden brown. Add about 1 cup of stock and whisk or stir to combine with the roux (it will clump up and you will think you've ruined it, but you haven't). Add another cup of stock and continue to whisk and the sauce should smooth out. Add the remaining stock and the thyme and oregano sprigs (or dried equivalents) and bring to a simmer.

7. Add the carrot and celery and simmer, uncovered, for 7 to 8 minutes, or until softened but not completely tender. Add the pearl onions and simmer for 2 minutes. »

8. While the vegetables cook, cut the chicken into bite-size pieces and get the dumpling dough out of the refrigerator.

9. Adjust the heat so that the sauce and vegetables are at a brisk simmer. Add the chicken pieces and the peas. Working as quickly as you can. use a small spoon to scoop out 1-tablespoon balls of dumpling dough and place evenly over the top of the sauce. Cover the Dutch oven, and cook for 18 minutes. Remove the lid and cut into a dumpling; the interior should be biscuit-like. If the interior is still doughy, cover the Dutch oven and cook for another minute or so.

10. When cooked through, remove from the heat, let cool for a few minutes, then ladle into two bowls.

TECHNIQUE TIP Dredging and frying the chicken is an unusual technique in chicken and dumplings, but I think the results are worth the time and effort it takes. However, if you're pressed for time, skip that step. Make the roux with plain flour and oil, and add cut-up chicken thighs with the carrots.

Sesame-Ginger Chicken with Snow Peas

ACTIVE TIME
30 MINUTES

TOTAL TIME
30 MINUTES

Serves 2

This recipe is based on a Taiwanese dish called "Three-Cup Chicken," but uses far less than the traditional 1:1:1 cup ratio of sesame oil, soy sauce, and rice wine. I also use boneless thighs, instead of harder-to-find bone-in chicken chunks. Overall, it's a light, delicious recipe.

1 cup snow peas, trimmed, strings removed

3 tablespoons sesame oil

1 (1-inch) piece of ginger, peeled and cut into thin coins

6 to 8 garlic cloves, peeled and cut in half

2 to 3 scallions, trimmed and cut into 1-inch pieces

½ teaspoon red pepper flakes

2 to 3 boneless skinless chicken thighs, each cut into 4 pieces

2 teaspoons sugar

⅓ cup rice wine or dry sherry

3 tablespoons soy sauce

¼ cup fresh Thai or regular basil leaves, torn into 2 to 3 pieces

1. Pour about 1 inch of water into the Dutch oven and place over high heat. Bring to a boil, then place a steamer basket filled with the snow peas in the pot. Cover and steam for 3 minutes, or until barely tender. Remove and set aside.

2. Empty the Dutch oven and wipe it dry. Place over medium heat and add the sesame oil. Heat until the oil thins out and shimmers. Add the ginger, garlic, scallions, and red pepper flakes, and cook, stirring, for 1 to 2 minutes or until very fragrant. Add the chicken pieces in a single layer, and cook for 2 minutes. Flip and cook the other side for 1 minute.

3. In a small bowl, whisk together the sugar, rice wine, and soy sauce. Add to the Dutch oven and bring to a simmer. Reduce the heat to medium-low and simmer, covered, for 10 minutes.

4. Remove the cover and stir. Cook, uncovered, for another 5 to 8 minutes, or until the chicken is tender. Stir in the snow peas and cook for 1 minute, just to heat the peas through. Stir in the basil and serve over rice.

Chicken Thighs
with White Beans and Prosciutto

ACTIVE TIME
40 MINUTES

TOTAL TIME
2 HOURS

Serves 2

Braising chicken thighs is a great way to cook them; the long slow heat breaks down the meat until it's moist and tender, almost silky. The only problem with traditional braised chicken is that the skin is soft instead of crisp. This two-step cooking method gets the best of both worlds: delicious braised meat and crisp skin.

2 to 3 tablespoons olive oil

2 to 4 bone-in, skin-on chicken thighs

Kosher salt

1 ounce prosciutto, diced
(2 to 3 thin slices or ¼ cup diced)

2 teaspoons minced garlic
(1 very large or 2 small cloves)

2 teaspoons finely minced
fresh rosemary, divided

⅓ cup dry white wine

¾ to 1 cup low-sodium chicken stock
(or more depending on pan size)

1 (15-ounce) can cannellini or other
white beans, drained and rinsed

1. Preheat the oven to 300°F.

2. Place the Dutch oven over medium heat. Add enough oil to coat the bottom of the pot and heat until the oil shimmers. While the oil is heating, season the skin-side of the chicken thighs with salt. When the oil is ready, carefully add the chicken, skin-side down, to the Dutch oven. Salt the other side of the thighs when they're in the pot. Cook without moving for 5 to 6 minutes, or until the thighs are golden brown. Turn and cook for another 3 to 5 minutes, or until the second side is browned. Transfer the chicken to a plate. Pour all but a thin coating of fat from the pan, and return it to the heat.

3. Add the prosciutto to the Dutch oven and cook, stirring, for 2 to 3 minutes, or until it begins to crisp. Add the garlic and half the rosemary, and cook for a minute or two, or until fragrant.

4. Pour in the wine and bring to a boil, scraping to release the browned bits from the bottom of the pan. Reduce the wine by half. Pour in ¾ cup of stock. Bring to a simmer and add the chicken thighs, skin-side up. The stock should come about halfway up the thighs; add more if needed.

5. Cover the Dutch oven and place it in the oven. Bake for 25 minutes. Remove the pot from the oven and turn the heat up to 400°F.

6. Remove the chicken thighs from the pot. If you have a fat separator, pour the sauce in and allow the fat to rise to the surface for 5 to 10 minutes. Pour the sauce back into the pot. If you don't have a fat separator, let the sauce sit for a few minutes to allow the fat to come to the surface, and skim or spoon off as much as possible.

7. Add the beans to the Dutch oven along with the remaining rosemary. Add the remaining ¼ cup of chicken stock and stir to coat the beans. Place the chicken thighs on the beans, skin-side up, and place the pot into the oven uncovered.

8. Bake for 15 minutes. Check to make sure the beans aren't too dry; they shouldn't be soupy but they should be coated generously with the sauce. If needed, add more stock. Return the pot to the oven and cook for another 5 to 10 minutes, or until the chicken skin is dark golden brown and crisp.

INGREDIENT TIP Chicken thighs can vary widely in size; if they are small, you'll probably want to cook four for this and similar recipes, but if they're large, 2 will probably be enough (unless you're counting on leftovers).

Chicken and Sausage Gumbo

ACTIVE TIME
30 MINUTES

TOTAL TIME
1 HOUR
10 MINUTES

Serves 2

Cajun cooks have several methods for making the roux that's the basis for gumbo. This is chef Paul Prudhomme's method, which involves 10 minutes of constant vigilance but results in lots of time saved. If you want to change the recipe up, you can substitute shrimp for the chicken; just add raw shrimp to the gumbo about 5 minutes before it's done cooking.

4 ounces Andouille sausage, diced

2 cups low-sodium chicken stock

3 tablespoons canola or vegetable oil

3 tablespoons all-purpose flour

½ cup chopped onion

⅓ cup chopped red bell pepper

1 small garlic clove, minced

1 small celery stalk, chopped (about ⅓ cup)

1 tablespoon tomato paste

1 tablespoon Worcestershire sauce

½ teaspoon dried oregano

½ teaspoon dried thyme

1 bay leaf

¼ teaspoon granulated garlic

⅛ teaspoon cayenne pepper

2 to 3 boneless chicken thighs, cut into bite-size pieces

1 cup cooked rice, for serving

1. Place the Dutch oven over medium heat and add the sausage. Cook, stirring occasionally, until it is browned and has rendered most of its fat. Remove the sausage and reserve. Add 1 cup of chicken stock and bring to a simmer, scraping up the browned bits from the bottom of the pot, so they don't burn. Pour off the stock, reserving for later.

2. Add the oil to the Dutch oven and turn the heat to medium-high. When the oil is shimmering, add the flour and whisk into the hot oil. Reduce the heat to medium and continue stirring for 6 minutes or so, until the roux turns a medium brown, the color of peanut butter. Add the onion and continue stirring for another 5 minutes or until the roux is a deep chocolate brown. Turn off the heat.

3. Add the bell pepper, garlic, celery, and tomato paste. Stir, cooking in the residual heat, for about 3 minutes, then add the reserved chicken stock. Turn the heat on and bring to a boil, then reduce to low. Add the reserved sausage, Worcestershire sauce, oregano, thyme, bay leaf, granulated garlic, cayenne, and chicken. Simmer, uncovered, for 20 to 30 minutes.

4. Scoop the rice into two bowls and serve the gumbo over it.

PERFECT PAIR I find that Cajun dishes like this one go better with beer than wine. Abita Brewing Company from Louisiana makes an amber beer that's a good match.

Farfalle and Chicken with Pesto Cream Sauce

ACTIVE TIME
20 MINUTES

TOTAL TIME
40 MINUTES

Serves 2

As in the recipe for Chicken and Herb Dumplings (page 118), I start the chicken for this recipe by dredging and frying the thighs. It can also easily be made with leftover cooked chicken; simply add it during the last step.

FOR THE PESTO

½ cup oil-packed sun-dried tomatoes (about 2½ ounces) plus 3 tablespoons of the oil

1 packed cup fresh basil leaves (about ½ ounce)

¼ cup grated Parmigiano-Reggiano (about 1 ounce)

1 garlic clove, minced

1 tablespoon toasted pine nuts

FOR THE PASTA

2 teaspoons kosher salt, plus more for sprinkling

6 ounces farfalle (butterfly or bowtie) pasta

2 boneless skinless chicken thighs

¼ cup all-purpose flour

2 to 3 tablespoons vegetable oil

⅓ cup dry white wine

¾ cup heavy cream

1. To make the pesto, place the sun-dried tomatoes and the oil, basil, cheese, garlic, and pine nuts in the bowl of a small food processor or small blender jar. Pulse until a coarse paste forms, adding a tablespoon or two of water if necessary to get a loose enough consistency. This should make about ¾ cup of pesto. The leftovers can be refrigerated for a week or so, or frozen for several months.

2. To make the farfalle, add 8 cups of water to the Dutch oven and place the pot over high heat. Add 2 teaspoons of salt and bring the water to a boil. Add the farfalle and cook according to the package directions. Drain, reserving at least 1 cup of the hot pasta water. Cover the water with a lid or plate to keep warm, and set both the water and the pasta aside.

3. While the water heats and the pasta cooks, sprinkle both sides of the chicken generously with salt. Place the flour in a shallow bowl and dredge the chicken to coat lightly. Set aside.

4. When the pasta is draining, wipe out the inside of the Dutch oven. Place the pot over medium heat and add enough oil to form a heavy coat. Heat until the oil shimmers, and add the chicken pieces. Cook without moving for 4 to 6 minutes, or until the chicken is golden brown. Turn and cook for another 4 minutes or until the second side is browned. Remove the chicken to a rack. Pour off the oil.

5. Turn the heat up to medium-high. Pour the wine into the Dutch oven and bring to a simmer, scraping up the browned bits from the bottom of the pot. Reduce by about half, then add the cream and bring to a boil. Cook for about 3 minutes, or until the cream has reduced by about one-third. Add the pesto and stir to combine.

6. While the wine and cream reduce, cut the chicken into bite-size pieces.

7. Pour the reserved hot pasta water over the cooked pasta to loosen it up, then add it to the sauce in the pot. Add the chicken and toss to coat the pasta with the sauce.

INGREDIENT TIP If you want to add vegetables to this dish, wilt a few handfuls of fresh spinach or arugula into the pasta during the last step.

Onion and Herb–Smothered Chicken

ACTIVE TIME
40 MINUTES

TOTAL TIME
2 HOURS

Serves 2

In traditional Southern cuisine, smothered chicken is browned and topped with creamy gravy filled with onions and, sometimes, other vegetables. This is lighter, and lets the flavor of the chicken and the onions shine through.

Kosher salt

2 or 3 chicken thigh-leg quarters

2 to 3 tablespoons unsalted butter

2 medium onions, peeled and cut into ¼-inch wedges

1 large or 2 small garlic cloves, minced

½ cup dry white wine

1 cup low-sodium chicken stock, or more

1 tablespoon all-purpose flour

½ teaspoon dried oregano, plus 1 teaspoon fresh leaves

½ teaspoon dried thyme, plus 1 teaspoon fresh leaves

1 small dried bay leaf

Freshly ground black pepper

1 teaspoon minced chives, for garnish (optional)

2 teaspoons chopped fresh parsley, for garnish (optional)

1. Preheat the oven to 300°F. Salt the chicken quarters on both sides and set aside while you prepare the rest of the ingredients.

2. Place the Dutch oven over medium heat. Add the butter. When the butter has just stopped foaming, add the chicken quarters, skin-side down. Cook for 5 to 6 minutes, or until golden brown. Turn and cook the other sides for 3 to 4 minutes, then transfer to a plate.

3. Pour off all but a light coating of fat from the Dutch oven. Add the onions and stir to coat with the oil. Sprinkle with salt and cook until the onion pieces just start to brown, about 4 minutes. Add the garlic and cook for a minute or two, or until fragrant. Add the wine and cook, scraping the bottom of the pan to dislodge the browned bits. Bring to a boil and reduce by about half.

4. In a small bowl, whisk together the chicken stock and flour and pour into the Dutch oven. Bring to a simmer and add the oregano, thyme, bay leaf, and pepper. Add the chicken quarters skin-side down. The liquid should come at least halfway up the sides of the chicken pieces; if not, add a little more stock.

5. Cover the pot and place in the oven. Bake for 25 minutes. Remove the pot from the oven and turn the oven up to 400°F.

6. Remove the chicken quarters from the pot. If you have a fat separator, strain the onions out and pour the sauce into the separator. Allow the fat to rise to the surface for 5 to 10 minutes. Pour the sauce back into the pot, adding the onions. If you don't have a fat separator, let the sauce sit for a few minutes to allow the fat to come to the surface of the Dutch oven, and skim or spoon off as much as possible.

7. Add the chicken quarters back to the Dutch oven, skin-side up. Return the pot to the oven, uncovered, and cook for another 20 to 25 minutes, or until the chicken skin is dark golden brown and crisp. Remove the chicken to plates, and stir in the fresh oregano and thyme. Spoon the sauce over the chicken and garnish with the additional herbs (if using).

TECHNIQUE TIP Chicken drumsticks feature several heavy tendons. I don't like them, so before cooking, I use sharp kitchen shears to cut through them. The meat shrinks up away from the bones, and is much easier to eat.

Chicken Braised with Red Bell Peppers and Paprika

ACTIVE TIME
40 MINUTES

TOTAL TIME
2 HOURS
10 MINUTES

Serves 2

A more modern take on Chicken Paprikash, this dish features red bell peppers in addition to the paprika. The chicken is braised in the oven rather than on the stove top, so the skin on the thighs stays crisper, which is always one of my goals when cooking chicken.

Kosher salt

2 to 4 bone-in, skin-on chicken thighs

2 to 3 tablespoons vegetable oil

½ small onion, sliced

1 small red bell pepper, seeded and cut into bite-size chunks

2 tablespoons ground sweet Hungarian paprika

1 cup low-sodium chicken stock (or more depending on pan size)

2 to 3 small red potatoes, cut into quarters

2 tablespoons sour cream

1 tablespoon chopped fresh parsley, plus more for garnish

1. Preheat the oven to 300°F. Salt the chicken thighs on both sides.

2. Place the Dutch oven over medium heat. Add enough oil to coat the bottom of the pot and heat until the oil shimmers. Carefully add the chicken, skin-side down. Cook without moving for 5 to 6 minutes, or until the thighs are golden brown. Turn and cook for another 3 to 5 minutes, or until the second side is browned. Transfer the chicken to a plate. Pour all but a thin coating of fat from the pan, and return it to the heat.

3. Add the onion and stir to coat with the oil. Sprinkle with salt and cook until the onion pieces soften and separate, about 3 minutes. Add the bell pepper and cook, stirring, for 2 to 3 minutes, or until they begin to soften. Add the paprika and stir to coat the vegetables. Cook for a minute or so, or until the paprika is fragrant but not burned.

4. Add the chicken stock and stir, scraping up the browned bits from the bottom of the pot. Bring to a simmer and add the chicken thighs, skin-side up. The stock should come at least halfway up the sides of the thighs; add more if necessary. Cover the pot, place it in the oven, and bake for 20 minutes.

5. Remove the pot from the oven and turn the heat up to 375°F. Take the chicken out of the pot and set aside.

6. If you have a fat separator, strain out the pepper and onion and reserve. Pour the sauce in and allow the fat to rise to the surface for 5 to 10 minutes. Pour the sauce back into the pot and add the pepper and onion. If you don't have a fat separator, let the sauce sit for a few minutes to allow the fat to come to the surface of the Dutch oven, and skim or spoon off as much as possible.

7. Add the potatoes to the pot and stir to coat with the sauce. Return the chicken to the pot, skin-side up. Bake, uncovered, for 20 minutes. Test a potato with a fork or skewer to make sure they're done; if not, return to the oven for another 5 to 10 minutes.

8. Take the pot out of the oven and remove the chicken and potatoes from the sauce. Stir the sour cream and parsley into the sauce and return the potatoes to the pot. Stir gently to coat with the sauce.

9. To serve, spoon the potatoes and sauce onto two plates. Place the chicken on top and garnish with additional parsley.

INGREDIENT TIP Traditionally, chicken paprikash is served with noodles (or spaetzle). If you prefer, leave out the potatoes and cook egg noodles while the chicken cooks. Stir them into the sauce after the sour cream is added.

Coq au Vin–Style Chicken Thighs

A true coq au vin is rarely made these days. First of all, it calls for a rooster (*coq*), which, being tough, needs long marinating and cooking time. Second, it requires cooking several elements separately to add to the finished dish. While I don't claim that this is a true coq au vin, it keeps all the good parts—bacon and red wine—and the Dutch oven does most of the work.

1 to 2 slices bacon, diced

2 to 4 bone-in chicken thighs

Kosher salt

½ very small onion, sliced (about ¼ cup)

1 garlic clove, sliced

1½ teaspoons tomato paste

1 cup dry red wine

⅓ cup chicken stock

½ teaspoon brown sugar

Freshly ground black pepper

1. Preheat the oven to 300°F.

2. Place the Dutch oven over medium heat. Add the bacon and stir to separate the pieces. Cook, stirring occasionally, until the bacon is crisp and has rendered most of its fat. Transfer the bacon pieces to a paper towel–lined plate, leaving the fat in the pot.

3. While the bacon cooks, sprinkle the skin-side of the chicken thighs with salt. When the bacon is out of the pot, carefully add the chicken, skin-side down, to the Dutch oven. Salt the other side of the thighs when they're in the pot. Cook without moving for 5 to 6 minutes, or until the thighs are golden brown. Turn and cook for another 3 to 5 minutes, or until the second side is browned. Transfer the chicken to a plate. Pour all but a thin coating of fat from the pan, and return it to the heat.

4. Add the onion and garlic to the Dutch oven and cook, stirring, for 2 to 3 minutes, or until the onion slices are beginning to soften and separate. Add the tomato paste and stir, breaking it up as much as possible. Cook for 2 to 3 minutes, or until it has darkened slightly.

5. Pour in the wine and bring to a boil, scraping to release the browned bits from the bottom of the pan. Reduce the wine by about half and add the stock and brown sugar, stirring to dissolve the sugar. Bring to a simmer and add the chicken thighs, skin-side up. The stock should come about halfway up the thighs; add more if needed.

6. Cover the Dutch oven and place it in the oven. Bake for 25 minutes. Remove the pot from the oven and turn the heat up to 400°F.

7. Remove the chicken thighs from the pot. If you have a fat separator, pour the sauce in and allow the fat to rise to the surface for 5 to 10 minutes. Pour the sauce back into the pot. If you don't have a fat separator, let the sauce sit for a few minutes to allow the fat to come to the surface of the Dutch oven, and skim or spoon off as much as possible.

8. Add the chicken thighs to the pot skin-side up and bake uncovered for 15 to 20 minutes, or until the chicken skin is golden brown and crisp and the sauce has thickened. Stir in the reserved bacon and serve with mashed potatoes or noodles, and season with the pepper.

PERFECT PAIR If you choose a young, unoaked Cabernet Sauvignon or blend to cook with, it will also be a good choice to pair with the dish.

Turkey Tenderloin Piccata

ACTIVE TIME
30 MINUTES

TOTAL TIME
30 MINUTES

Serves 2

Turkey tenderloins are perfect for this dish. The tenderloin, which is a strip of boneless turkey breast, is a great cut for two, because it's much smaller than a whole or even half breast. Since it's boneless, it's easy to cut and pound for this dish, which comes together very quickly.

1 (12-ounce) turkey tenderloin

Kosher salt

Freshly ground black pepper

½ cup all-purpose flour

2 to 3 tablespoons olive oil

3 tablespoons unsalted butter, divided

1 medium shallot, finely chopped

¼ cup white wine

3 tablespoons freshly squeezed lemon juice

1 tablespoon capers, drained

2 tablespoons chopped fresh parsley

1. Preheat a warming drawer or oven to 170°F.

2. Cut the turkey tenderloin crosswise (against the grain) into ½-inch slices. Place the slices between two pieces of heavy plastic wrap (or in a large heavy plastic bag). Use a meat mallet if you have one, or a small heavy skillet if you don't, to gently pound the slices to ⅛-inch thick. Season the turkey slices on both sides with salt and pepper. In a shallow bowl, place the flour and dredge the turkey slices to coat both sides lightly.

3. Place the Dutch oven over medium heat. Add enough oil to coat the bottom of the pot and heat until the oil shimmers. Add 1 tablespoon of butter. When it's foaming, add the turkey slices in a single layer (you may have to work in batches) and cook without moving for 1 to 2 minutes or until lightly browned. Cook for 1 minute on the second side. Remove to a rack and place in the warming drawer or warm oven.

4. To the Dutch oven, add the shallot and cook, stirring, for 2 to 3 minutes, or until softened and just starting to brown. Pour in the wine and lemon juice and bring to a simmer, stirring to get up any browned bits from the bottom of the pot. Turn the heat off and stir in the capers. Let the Dutch oven cool for several minutes, then stir in the butter, 1 tablespoon at a time. Stir in the parsley.

5. Remove the turkey from the oven and transfer to a plate. Drizzle the sauce over and serve immediately.

INGREDIENT TIP You can use boneless chicken breasts in this recipe instead of turkey. Be careful pounding them; the meat is a little softer than turkey so it tears more easily.

Ancho Chile–Braised Turkey Thighs

ACTIVE TIME
40 MINUTES

TOTAL TIME
2 HOURS
30 MINUTES

Serves 2

If you've ever had beef barbacoa tacos at Chipotle, this sauce will seem familiar. While it's great for braised beef, I think it really brings out the best in poultry, and since turkey thighs take so well to braising, it's a natural match. Once you have the sauce made, the thighs cook mostly unattended.

1 ounce dried ancho chiles
(3 to 5 chiles)

2 to 3 tablespoons vegetable oil

1 medium onion, sliced (about 1 cup)

2 garlic cloves, peeled and smashed

Kosher salt

½ cup mild beer

1 chipotle chile in adobo sauce

½ teaspoon dried oregano

½ teaspoon ground cumin

1½ teaspoons sugar

2 tablespoons apple cider vinegar

1 large or two small turkey thighs, skin removed

Tortillas (optional)

Avocado slices (optional)

Pickled red onion (optional)

Rice (optional)

1. Preheat the oven to 300°F.

2. Remove the stems and seeds from the ancho chiles and tear or cut into wide strips. Fill a medium bowl with several cups of very hot tap water and place it near the stove.

3. Place the Dutch oven over medium heat. Add enough oil to coat the bottom of the pot and heat until the oil shimmers. A few at a time, add the strips of chiles and cook for a minute on both sides, until they're fragrant. After cooking, submerge the chile strips in the water. Repeat with the rest of the chiles. Let the chiles rehydrate for 15 minutes or so while you prepare the rest of the sauce.

4. With the Dutch oven still over medium heat, add the onion and garlic and season with salt. Cook, stirring occasionally, for 4 to 6 minutes, or until quite browned. Pour the beer into the pan and scrape the bottom of the pot to get up the browned bits. Bring to a boil and reduce the liquid by about half.

5. Pour the onion mixture into the jar of a blender. Add the chiles and 1½ cups of the soaking liquid, the chipotle, oregano, cumin, sugar, vinegar, and 2 teaspoons of salt. Blend on high until smooth and pour back into the Dutch oven. Place the Dutch oven over medium heat and bring the sauce to a simmer. Add the turkey thighs, turning to coat with the sauce.

6. In the covered pot, cook the thighs for 90 minutes then check to see if the meat is tender. If not, continue cooking for another 30 minutes (large thighs will usually take the entire 2 hours).

7. When the thighs are tender, remove them from the sauce and set aside to cool. If the sauce has much fat floating on the surface and you have a fat separator, pour the sauce into the separator and let it sit for 10 minutes or so. Pour the sauce back into the Dutch oven, leaving the fat behind in the separator. If the sauce doesn't have much fat or you don't have a separator, simply blot or spoon up any fat from the surface.

8. When the thighs are cool enough to handle, tear or cut the meat off the bones and return to the sauce. Warm the meat and sauce through. Serve the meat with a little of the sauce in tortillas garnished with avocado slices and pickled onions (if using), or spoon it over steamed rice (if using). Leftovers are great in enchiladas.

TECHNIQUE TIP You'll have extra sauce after cooking the thighs. It can be refrigerated for several days or frozen for up to a month. Use it to braise more turkey, chicken thighs, or pork country-style ribs, or use it in chili or as an enchilada sauce.

Braised Duck Quarters in Savory Orange Sauce

ACTIVE TIME
20 MINUTES

TOTAL TIME
2 HOURS

Serves 2

Americans don't cook much duck, but if you've never tried it, you owe it to yourself to take the plunge. The braising liquid in this recipe is based on a sauce we developed for duck breasts for a Valentine's Day class. Lillet is a vermouth-like aperitif wine, with herbal and citrus notes that complement the duck nicely. Make sure you get the blanc and not the rouge or rosé. If you can't find it, use dry vermouth instead.

2 duck leg-thigh quarters (about 1¼ pounds)

Kosher salt

2 to 3 tablespoons olive or vegetable oil

1 small shallot, sliced

½ cup Lillet blanc or dry white vermouth

½ cup orange juice

1 tablespoon sherry vinegar

½ cup low-sodium chicken stock

1 sprig fresh thyme (or ½ teaspoon dried)

1. Season the duck quarters on both sides with kosher salt. Let sit for 20 minutes up to an hour. Blot any moisture off with paper towels before searing.

2. Preheat the oven to 325°F.

3. Place the Dutch oven over medium heat. Add enough oil to coat the bottom of the pot and heat until the oil shimmers. Add the duck quarters, skin-side down, and brown without moving for 5 to 6 minutes, or until golden brown. Turn the quarters over and brown on the other side, another 4 minutes or so. Transfer the duck pieces to a plate. Pour off all but about 1 tablespoon of the fat in the pot.

4. Add the shallot to the Dutch oven and sprinkle with a pinch of salt. Cook, stirring, until the shallot just begins to brown, about 3 minutes. Pour in the Lillet and bring to a simmer, scraping the bottom of the pan to get up the browned bits. Reduce the Lillet by about half. Add the orange juice, sherry vinegar, and chicken stock and stir to combine. Bring to a simmer and add the duck quarters, skin-side up. Push the thyme sprig into the liquid (or stir in the dried thyme, if using). Cover the Dutch oven.

5. Place the pot in the oven and bake for 75 to 90 minutes, or until the duck is quite tender and pulling away from the bones (depending on the size of the duck quarters, this could take up to 2 hours).

6. Remove the duck from the sauce. If you have a fat separator, strain the solids from the liquid and pour the sauce into the separator. Allow the fat to rise to the surface for 5 to 10 minutes and pour the sauce and the solids back into the pot. If you don't have a fat separator, let the sauce sit for a few minutes to allow the fat to come to the surface of the Dutch oven, and skim or spoon off as much as possible.

7. If the sauce is too thin, place the Dutch oven over medium heat and bring it to a simmer. Reduce until it's the consistency of gravy.

8. To serve, place one duck quarter on each plate and spoon the warm sauce over it.

PERFECT PAIR Wondering what else to do with Lillet? Try serving it as a refreshing aperitif while you wait for the duck to cook: Fill a rocks glass with ice and pour in several ounces of the Lillet. Top with club soda and garnish with an orange slice.

MEAT

chapter seven

Italian Pork Sandwiches with Broccoli Rabe

ACTIVE TIME
35 MINUTES

TOTAL TIME
2 HOURS
30 MINUTES

Serves 2

I have a confession to make: I've never tasted the original version of this sandwich, which hails from Philadelphia. But my version gets rave reviews from guests who have tried the sandwich in Philly. To be authentic, the broccoli rabe should be sautéed in garlic and placed on top of the pork, but this method saves a pan—and some time.

1 pound bone-in (or ¾ pound boneless) pork country shoulder ribs

Kosher salt

6 ounces broccoli rabe, about ⅓ to ½ bunch

2 to 3 tablespoons olive oil

1 small onion, sliced thin

4 large garlic cloves, minced

½ cup red wine

1 cup chicken stock

1 teaspoon fennel seeds

1 teaspoon dried thyme

1 bay leaf

¾ teaspoon red pepper flakes

¼ teaspoon freshly ground black pepper

1 sprig fresh rosemary

1 sprig fresh parsley (including the stems)

2 to 3 ounces sharp provolone cheese, about 4 slices, sliced thin

2 hoagie rolls, split almost all the way through but not quite

Sliced pickled peppers (optional)

1. Season all sides of the country ribs with salt and let rest while you cook the broccoli rabe.

2. Add 8 cups of water to the Dutch oven and place the pot over high heat. Add 2 teaspoons of salt and bring the water to a boil. While the water heats, trim ¼-inch from the ends of the broccoli rabe. Cut the stems from the leaves and any florets. Cut the stems on the diagonal into pieces about ¾-inch long and cut the leaves into thick ribbons (about 1-inch thick). When the water comes to a boil, add the stems and cook for 2 minutes. Add the leaves and florets and cook for 1 minute. Drain and rinse with cold water to stop the cooking. Set aside. Dry the inside of the Dutch oven.

3. Preheat the oven to 300°F.

4. Place the Dutch oven over medium heat. Add enough oil to coat the bottom of the pot and heat until the oil shimmers. Add the pork and brown for about 2 minutes without moving. When the first side is browned, turn and brown another side. Transfer to a plate.

5. Add the onion to the Dutch oven and sprinkle with salt. Stir to coat with the oil, then cook for 3 to 4 minutes, or until the onion slices begin to brown. Add the garlic and cook, stirring, for 1 to 2 minutes or until fragrant. Add the red wine and bring to a boil, scraping the bottom of the pot to dislodge any browned bits. Reduce the wine by about half, then add the stock, fennel seeds, thyme, bay leaf, red pepper flakes, black pepper, rosemary, and parsley. Add the pork to the pot and bring to a simmer.

6. Bake, covered, for 90 minutes to 2 hours, or until the pork shreds easily with a fork. Remove the pork from the Dutch oven and transfer to a plate. Remove the rosemary and parsley stems and the bay leaf.

7. If you have a fat separator, pour the sauce in, straining out the solids, and allow the fat to rise to the surface for 5 to 10 minutes. Pour the sauce and the solids back into the pot. If you don't have a fat separator, let the sauce sit for a few minutes to allow the fat to come to the surface of the Dutch oven, and skim off as much as possible.

8. When the meat is cool enough to handle, shred it into bite-size chunks, discarding any gristle. Return the meat to the Dutch oven and place it over medium heat. Bring the sauce to a simmer and stir to coat the meat. If the sauce is watery, bring it to a boil and reduce it for 3 to 4 minutes. It should look like thin gravy. Add the broccoli rabe and stir to heat through.

9. Layer the provolone slices over both sides of the rolls and spoon the meat and broccoli rabe mixture into the rolls. If you like, garnish the sandwiches with sliced pickled peppers, either hot or mild.

Roasted Italian Sausages with Fennel, Onion, and Oranges

ACTIVE TIME
30 MINUTES

TOTAL TIME
1 HOUR
15 MINUTES

Serves 2

I got the idea for the roasted fennel and onions with oranges from a recipe by cookbook author Molly Stevens. Here, my adaptation of her recipe becomes a main dish with the addition of Italian sausages.

2 to 4 mild or hot Italian sausages

1 small bulb fennel (or ½ large bulb)

½ small red onion

2 to 3 tablespoons olive oil

Kosher salt

1 naval orange

Freshly ground black pepper

1. Preheat the oven to 375°F.

2. Add about 1½ inches of water to the Dutch oven and place over high heat. When the water is simmering, turn down the heat to keep the water at a low simmer and add the Italian sausages. Cook for 8 minutes. Remove and drain. Pour the water out of the Dutch oven and wipe dry.

3. Meanwhile trim the root and any stems or fronds off the fennel. Cut out the core from the bottom center of the bulb, and slice into pieces about ¼-inch thick. Cut the onion into ¼-inch wedges.

4. Add the fennel and onion to the Dutch oven and drizzle with enough oil to coat the vegetables. Season generously with salt. Toss well to combine.

5. Place the sausages on top of the vegetables and roast, uncovered, for 15 minutes.

6. While the vegetables and sausages are roasting, prepare the orange. Use a rasp style grater such as a Microplane to remove about 1 teaspoon of the zest and set aside. With a sharp knife, cut off the ends of the orange and slice off the peel and pith. Cut into segments by slicing on either side of each piece of membrane to release the slices. Work over a bowl to save the juice.

7. Remove the pot from the oven. Move the sausages to the sides of the pot and toss the vegetables; they should be getting browned in spots. Move the sausages back to the center of the Dutch oven, turning them over. Roast for another 10 to 15 minutes, or until the vegetables and sausages are browned. Remove the pot from the oven. Remove the sausages and set aside.

8. Add the orange segments and zest to the fennel and onion mixture. Drizzle with about 2 tablespoons of the juice and toss gently. Spoon the vegetable mixture onto two plates and top with the sausages.

Pork Chops with Braised Cabbage and Apples

ACTIVE TIME
20 MINUTES

TOTAL TIME
55 MINUTES

Serves 2

With her German heritage, my mom often braised red cabbage with apples for dinner, and usually served it with pork chops. Today's leaner pork requires more care. I cook the chops with the cabbage, which helps keep them juicy while flavoring the cabbage.

2 ¾-inch thick rib (preferred) or loin pork chops

Kosher salt

2 to 3 tablespoons butter

½ small onion, sliced (about ½ cup)

4 cups sliced red cabbage (about ½ a small cabbage head)

½ small Granny Smith apple, peeled, cored, and chopped

½ cup low-sodium chicken stock

1 tablespoon brown sugar

½ teaspoon caraway seeds

2 tablespoons cider vinegar

Freshly ground black pepper

Noodles or mashed potatoes (optional)

1. Preheat the oven to 300°F.

2. Season the chops with salt on both sides. Place the Dutch oven over medium heat. Add enough butter to form a light coating on the bottom of the pot. When the butter has just stopped foaming, add the pork chops and cook without moving for 3 minutes, or until lightly browned. Turn and cook the other side for 2 to 3 minutes, or until browned. Remove the chops to a plate.

3. With the Dutch oven still over medium heat, add the onion, cabbage, and apple and stir to coat with the butter. Sprinkle with salt and cook for 2 to 3 minutes, or until the vegetables have softened somewhat. Add the chicken stock, brown sugar, caraway seeds, and cider vinegar and bring to a simmer.

4. Add the pork chops to the pot, nestling them into the cabbage so that they are mostly submerged.

5. Bake, covered, for 15 minutes. Remove the lid and bake for another 10 minutes, or until the cabbage is tender and the pork chops are cooked through. Remove the pot from the oven. If there is too much liquid in the cabbage, bring it to a simmer over medium heat to reduce the liquid.

6. Serve the chops and cabbage, season with black pepper, and serve over noodles or mashed potatoes, if desired.

INGREDIENT TIP Rib chops generally stay juicier than loin chops, so if you all you can find is loin chops (sometimes called "center cut" chops), you may wish to brine them. Dissolve ½ cup kosher salt (or ¼ cup fine salt) in 2 cups hot water, then stir in 2 cups ice water. Soak the chops for 2 to 3 hours then remove and pat dry. Don't salt the chops before searing them.

Pork Fried Rice with Peas and Mushrooms

ACTIVE TIME
25 MINUTES

TOTAL TIME
25 MINUTES

Serves 2

Fried rice is a great master recipe, since the basic method lends itself to using just about any leftover cooked meat or vegetables you might have in the fridge. You can make a vegetarian version by leaving out the pork and doubling up on the mushrooms and eggs.

2 cups cooked rice

6 ounces white or cremini mushrooms

2 tablespoons vegetable oil, plus 1 tablespoon

Kosher salt

¼ pound ground pork

1 tablespoon minced garlic

1 tablespoon minced ginger

2 or 3 scallions, diced (about ½ cup)

½ small red bell pepper, diced (about ½ cup)

½ cup frozen thawed peas

1 egg, beaten

2 tablespoons soy sauce

1 tablespoon rice vinegar

2 teaspoons toasted sesame oil

1 teaspoon Asian chili sauce or Sriracha sauce (optional)

1. If the rice is refrigerated, bring it to room temperature, breaking up any clumps.

2. Wash the mushrooms and trim the stems off; reserve them. Quarter the mushrooms if small to medium; cut into eighths if they are large. Pile the mushrooms in the Dutch oven and cover with just enough water to make the mushrooms float. Add about 2 tablespoons of oil and sprinkle generously with salt. Place the pot over high heat and bring to a boil. Continue boiling until the water has all evaporated and you can hear the mushrooms begin to sizzle. When you hear them sizzling, let them brown on one side, then flip with a spatula to brown the other sides.

3. Move the mushrooms to the sides of the Dutch oven and turn the heat down to medium-high. Add the pork, garlic, and ginger. Cook, stirring to break up the pork, until it is no longer pink. Add the scallions and red bell pepper and cook for 2 to 3 minutes, or until the vegetables soften. Add the rice and peas and stir to combine.

4. Move the rice mixture to the perimeter of the Dutch oven. Pour the remaining 1 tablespoon of vegetable oil in the middle and let it heat until it shimmers. Pour in the egg and stir to scramble. Cook just until done. Mix the rice into the egg and add the soy sauce, vinegar, sesame oil, and chili sauce (if using). Serve immediately.

TECHNIQUE TIP Fried rice actually works best with rice that's a day or so old, so it's the perfect way to use up leftovers. If you're making rice for another dish earlier in the week, cook extra and save it for this recipe.

Stir-Fried Pork with Tangerines and Bok Choy

ACTIVE TIME
35 MINUTES

TOTAL TIME
35 MINUTES

Serves 2

A combination of tender pork, tangy clementines, and sweet and spicy sauce makes this dish a winner in my book. It also cooks quickly, a plus on busy weeknights.

FOR THE PORK

1 (¾-pound) pork tenderloin, trimmed, cut crosswise into ½-inch-thick rounds, then cut into ½-inch-wide strips

Kosher salt

Freshly ground black pepper

2 teaspoons cornstarch

2 to 3 small seedless tangerines or clementines

5 scallions

Vegetable oil

1 teaspoon minced fresh ginger

3 baby bok choy, cut crosswise into 1-inch-thick ribbons, tough bases discarded

FOR THE SAUCE

¼ cup Thai sweet chili sauce

¼ cup chicken stock

½ teaspoon cornstarch

1 tablespoon soy sauce

2 teaspoons toasted sesame oil

¼ teaspoon Chinese five-spice powder

1. Place the pork tenderloin strips in a medium bowl; season with salt and pepper and toss with cornstarch to coat.

2. Remove about 2 teaspoons of the tangerine zest with a rasp-style grater such as a Microplane, then peel and section the tangerines. Cut the white parts of the scallions into 1-inch pieces and thinly slice the greens on the diagonal. Set the greens aside for a garnish.

3. Make the sauce. In a small bowl, whisk the chili sauce, stock, cornstarch, soy sauce, sesame oil, and five-spice powder together, along with the tangerine zest.

4. Pour enough oil into the bottom of the Dutch oven to form a heavy coat, and heat over medium-high heat until it shimmers. Add the pork tenderloin strips in one layer; stir-fry until the pork is brown and almost cooked through, about 3 minutes. Remove and set aside.

5. Lower the heat to medium and add the ginger, the white part of the scallions, and the bok choy and sauté for 3 to 4 minutes, until the vegetables are just starting to brown. Add the tangerine pieces; toss for about 30 seconds, just to warm through.

6. Add the sauce and bring to a simmer; cook for 2 to 3 minutes until the sauce thickens. Add the meat back to the Dutch oven. Season with salt and pepper. Garnish with sliced scallion greens and serve over rice or Chinese noodles (if using).

SEASONAL SWAP If it's not the season for tangerines, you can substitute navel orange segments and zest. The flavor is a little different, but still delicious. Depending on the size of the orange, you may wish to cut the segments in half.

Seared Pork Medallions with Sweet and Pickled Peppers

ACTIVE TIME
30 MINUTES

TOTAL TIME
30 MINUTES

Serves 2

This dish was inspired by a recipe from Bruce Aidells' *Great Meat Cookbook*, which pairs pork chops with sage and peppers. I find that pork tenderloin, when cooked quickly, retains more moisture than chops, and I add a little butter-enriched sauce for even more flavor. If you can't find sweet cherry peppers, you can substitute any mild pickled pepper.

1 (12-ounce) pork tenderloin

Kosher salt

Freshly ground black pepper

Vegetable oil

½ cup dry white wine

2 teaspoons pickling liquid from the peppers

½ cup chicken stock

2 teaspoons finely minced fresh rosemary leaves

2 medium garlic cloves, finely minced (about 2 teaspoons)

1 small roasted red bell pepper, cut into strips

5 to 6 pickled sweet cherry peppers, stems and seeds removed, then quartered

2 teaspoons butter

1. Slice the pork into medallions about 1½-inches thick. Use the palm of your hand to flatten the medallions to about ¾-inch. Season liberally on both sides with salt and pepper.

2. Place the Dutch oven over medium heat. Add enough oil to coat the bottom of the pot and heat until the oil shimmers. Add the pork medallions and cook until deep golden brown on both sides, about 6 to 7 minutes total. Transfer to a plate or a rack over a small sheet pan. Cover loosely with aluminum foil.

3. Add the wine and pickling liquid to the pot and turn the heat up to medium-high. Bring the liquid to a boil, scraping up any browned bits, and cook until reduced by about half. Add the stock, rosemary, and garlic and again bring to a boil to reduce by about half. Add the roasted bell pepper and pickled pepper strips and stir to heat through.

4. Remove the Dutch oven from the heat and let cool for a minute or two. One teaspoon at a time, swirl in the butter to thicken the sauce. Add the pork medallions and turn over to coat with the sauce and reheat.

INGREDIENT TIP You can either use a roasted pepper from a jar or roast your own. To roast, cut the pepper in half and remove the stem and seeds. Place it skin-side up on a small sheet pan and broil until charred. Cover the pepper pieces or wrap in foil to steam for a few minutes; peel the skin off. You can refrigerate or freeze any extra peppers.

Beef Daube Provençal

ACTIVE TIME
30 MINUTES

TOTAL TIME
3 HOURS
PLUS
MARINATING TIME

Serves 2

Daubes are different from other stews. Uncooked meat is marinated in a wine-based mixture overnight before slowly braising with bacon and vegetables. You also don't brown the meat. It takes advance planning, but it actually requires less hands-on attention than other stews. The potatoes are not traditional, but a daube is often served over them, so I add them to the stew. If you want to be authentic, leave them out and serve over mashed potatoes or noodles.

2 to 3 small red potatoes, cut into quarters

2 to 3 tablespoons olive oil

1 small onion, sliced

2 garlic cloves, peeled and mashed

1 celery stalk, sliced thin

½ cup dry white wine

2 tablespoons brandy

1 teaspoon kosher salt

¼ teaspoon freshly ground black pepper

1 fresh thyme sprig

1 bay leaf, crumbled

1 pound beef shoulder (chuck), cut into 2-inch cubes and trimmed of fat

2 to 3 slices bacon or pancetta, cut into batons ¼-inch wide by 1-inch long

1 large carrot, peeled and thinly sliced

1 large tomato, seeded and diced

¼ to ½ cup beef stock

2 tablespoons chopped fresh parsley

1. Add ½-inch of water to the Dutch oven and bring to a boil over high heat. Place the potatoes in a steamer basket. When the water is boiling, add the steamer basket and cover the Dutch oven. Cook for 15 minutes, or until the potatoes are mostly tender but still somewhat firm. Remove and cool. Refrigerate until ready to use. Empty the Dutch oven and dry the interior.

2. Place the Dutch oven over medium heat. Add enough oil to coat the bottom of the pot and heat until the oil shimmers. Add the onion, garlic, and celery and cook, stirring, 3 to 4 minutes, until softened. Add the wine and brandy and bring to a boil. Cook for a minute, then turn the heat off and pour the mixture into a bowl to cool.

3. When cool, stir in the salt and pepper. Pour the wine and vegetable mixture into a large sealable plastic bag and add the thyme, bay leaf, and beef. Seal the bag and refrigerate 4 hours to overnight.

4. When you're ready to cook the daube, preheat the oven to 350°F.

5. Add half the bacon or pancetta to the bottom of the Dutch oven. Add the meat, vegetables, and marinade from the bag. Top with the carrot and tomato and sprinkle with the rest of the bacon. The ingredients should not be covered with liquid, but you should be able to see liquid coming about one-third of the way up the ingredients. Add beef stock as needed. Cover the pot and place in the oven.

6. Cook for 30 minutes, then turn the heat down to 300°F. Cook for 90 minutes to 2 hours, or until the beef is tender enough to fall apart when probed with a fork. Add the potatoes and cover the pot. Cook for another 20 minutes or so, or until the potatoes are tender.

7. Let the daube cool for 15 minutes, then skim or blot off any fat on the surface. Ladle into bowls and garnish with the chopped parsley.

TECHNIQUE TIP It might seem odd to precook the potatoes rather than just throw them into the daube earlier, but the acid from the wine will keep them too firm unless they're partially steamed or parboiled.

Beef and Onions Braised in Porter

ACTIVE TIME
35 MINUTES

TOTAL TIME
2 HOURS
15 MINUTES

Serves 2

Formally known as *Carbonnade Flamande*, this rich Belgian beef stew is flavored with thyme, beer, onions, and mustard. Since it's Belgian in origin, traditionally you would use a Belgian dark beer in the sauce. I find Belgian dark beers to be a little too sour for my taste, and the reduction during cooking intensifies that effect. I prefer porter or stout, which tend to be sweeter. If you use a Belgian dark beer, you may want to increase the brown sugar.

1 pound boneless beef shoulder (chuck), cut into 2-inch-wide strips

Kosher salt

2 to 3 tablespoons vegetable oil

1 large onion, sliced (about 1½ cups)

¼ teaspoon dried thyme

8 ounces porter or other dark beer

⅓ cup low-sodium beef stock

½ teaspoon Dijon-style mustard

½ teaspoon brown sugar (or more)

1. Preheat the oven to 300°F. Sprinkle the pieces of beef with salt.

2. Place the Dutch oven over medium heat. Add enough oil to coat the bottom of the pot and heat until the oil shimmers and flows like water. Add the pieces of beef and cook without moving for 3 to 4 minutes, or until browned. Turn and brown at least one other side of the strips, then remove to a plate.

3. Add the onion to the Dutch oven and sprinkle with salt and the thyme. Cook, stirring, for 4 to 5 minutes, or just until the onion starts to brown. Add the porter and stir, scraping up any browned bits from the bottom of the pot. Bring to a boil and reduce by about one-quarter.

4. Add the beef stock, mustard, and sugar and stir to dissolve the sugar. Bring to a simmer and add the beef back to the Dutch oven.

5. Cook, covered, for 75 to 90 minutes, or until the beef pulls apart with a fork. Take the pieces of beef out of the Dutch oven and place on a rack to cool. If you have a fat separator, strain the onion from the liquid and pour the sauce into the separator. Allow the fat to rise to the surface for 5 to 10 minutes and pour the sauce and the onion back into the pot. If you don't have a fat separator, let the sauce sit for a few minutes to allow the fat to come to the surface of the Dutch oven, and skim or spoon off as much as possible.

6. Place the Dutch oven over medium heat and bring the sauce to a simmer. Cook for 5 to 10 minutes, or until the sauce has thickened to the consistency of gravy. Add the beef back to the sauce to heat up. If you like, serve it over mashed potatoes.

PERFECT PAIR Pairing this dish with more of the beer you used in the recipe is a natural, but it's also delicious with a full-bodied red wine, such as an old-vine Zinfandel.

Pot Roast for Two (Really!)

Pot roast is comfort food at its finest. But it usually serves six to eight people or more. The trick to cooking pot roast for two is finding the right cut of beef. It can be difficult to find a small piece of chuck that's thick enough. We often buy a large piece of boneless chuck (2½ to 4 pounds) and divide it into two or three portions, freezing the rest for future meals.

1 pound beef chuck (shoulder) roast, preferably 2 inches thick

Kosher salt

Freshly ground black pepper

2 to 3 tablespoons vegetable oil

1 tablespoon tomato paste

1½ cups low-sodium beef stock

¼ cup red wine

½ teaspoon Worcestershire sauce

3 to 4 boiling onions (about 1½ inches in diameter), peeled and cut in half through the root

2 large carrots, peeled and cut into 2-inch lengths

¼ pound small red or Yukon Gold potatoes, left whole if 1 to 1½ inches in diameter, cut in half if larger.

1. Preheat the oven to 325°F.

2. Season the roast on all sides with 1 teaspoon of salt and a generous grinding of pepper.

3. Place the Dutch oven over medium heat. Add enough oil to coat the bottom of the pot and heat until the oil shimmers. Brown the roast on all sides, about 8 minutes total. Transfer the roast to a plate. Add the tomato paste and cook, stirring, until the paste has darkened slightly, about 1 minute. Stir in the beef broth, wine, and Worcestershire sauce and stir, scraping the bottom of the cooker to get up any browned bits. Bring to a simmer. Place the roast in the liquid and cover the pot.

4. Cook for 1 hour. Remove from the oven and add the onions, carrots, and potatoes. Continue to cook, covered, for 30 to 40 more minutes, or until the beef and vegetables are tender.

5. Transfer the roast to a cutting board and tent with aluminum foil for 15 minutes to rest. If there is a large amount of fat in the sauce, pour it into a fat separator and let the fat rise to the surface, then return the sauce to the pan. If it's very thin, you may want to simmer it so it reduces slightly. Taste and adjust seasoning, adding salt, pepper or more Worcestershire sauce if necessary.

6. Slice the roast into thick pieces, going against the grain. Arrange the vegetables and meat on a serving tray and pour the sauce over the top.

Chinese Pepper Steak Stir-Fry

ACTIVE TIME
25 MINUTES

TOTAL TIME
25 MINUTES

Serves 2

Cooking a stir-fry dish in a Dutch oven requires a different procedure than a wok, but it works quite well once you get the hang of it. Since you can't move cooked food to the relatively cooler sides of a hot wok, you need to work in stages. It takes a little longer, but the advantage is that you can get all the ingredients cooked perfectly before combining with the sauce.

FOR THE STEAK

1 (8-ounce) sirloin steak, flat iron steak, flap meat, or flank steak

2 teaspoons soy sauce

¼ cup dry sherry, plus 2 teaspoons

2 scallions, divided

3 to 4 tablespoons vegetable oil

½ medium red bell pepper, seeded and cut into bite-size pieces

½ medium green bell pepper, seeded and cut into bite-size pieces

1 small onion, cut into eight wedges

1 jalapeño pepper, seeded and cut into thin strips (optional)

2 teaspoons minced garlic (1 to 2 cloves)

2 teaspoons minced fresh ginger (about a 1-inch piece)

FOR THE SAUCE

3 tablespoons light soy sauce

3 tablespoons rice vinegar

⅓ cup low-sodium beef or chicken stock

1 tablespoon toasted sesame oil

1 tablespoon sugar

1½ teaspoons freshly ground black pepper

1 teaspoon cornstarch

1. Slice the steak against the grain into pieces about ¼-inch thick. In a medium bowl, toss the steak strips with the soy sauce and 2 teaspoons of sherry.

2. Dice the white parts of the scallions and thinly slice the greens on the diagonal. Set the greens aside for a garnish.

3. For the sauce, in a small bowl, whisk all of the ingredients together. Set aside.

4. Pour enough oil into the bottom of the Dutch oven to form a light coat, and heat over medium-high heat until it shimmers. Add the bell pepper chunks and cook without stirring for about 2 minutes, so that the pieces brown in spots. Stir and cook for 2 to 3 more minutes, or until the peppers are browned on most sides but not charred.

5. Add the onion wedges and cook, stirring, until they brown slightly, about 2 minutes. Add the jalapeño (if using) and cook another minute. Remove all the vegetables to a bowl. There should be enough oil to form a thin coat in the pot; if not, add a little more and heat it until it shimmers.

6. Add the steak strips in one layer and cook for 1 to 2 minutes, or until the first side is browned. Turn the strips over with tongs or a spatula to brown the other side. The beef should be deep brown and almost cooked through. Transfer to a bowl and set aside.

7. Add the garlic, ginger, and the white parts of the scallions to the Dutch oven and stir for a minute or so, just until fragrant. Add the remaining ¼ cup of sherry and stir, scraping to get up the browned bits from the bottom of the pot. Whisk the sauce and add it to the pot. Bring the mixture to a simmer and cook for 2 to 3 minutes or until thickened slightly. Return the vegetables and beef to the pot and stir to warm up and coat with the sauce. Serve over cooked rice, if desired, and garnish with the reserved scallion greens.

Hoisin–Braised Beef

ACTIVE TIME
15 MINUTES

TOTAL TIME
1 HOUR,
15 MINUTES

Serves 2

Hoisin sauce is a sweet and spicy sauce used in Southern Chinese cooking. It's made with soybeans, sugar, vinegar, garlic, and spices that lend depth and richness. It features prominently in this braising liquid, which is one of my standards. It is very versatile and I use it with cubes of pork shoulder, or chicken or turkey thighs (left whole, skin removed).

2 to 3 tablespoons vegetable oil

1 pound beef shoulder (chuck), cut into ¾-inch cubes and trimmed of fat

¼ cup dry sherry

¼ cup hoisin sauce

2 tablespoons rice vinegar

2 tablespoons soy sauce

¼ cup orange juice

1 tablespoon minced fresh ginger

2 teaspoons minced garlic

½ teaspoon red pepper flakes

1. Preheat the oven to 300°F.

2. Place the Dutch oven over medium heat. Add enough oil to coat the bottom of the pot and heat until the oil shimmers. Add half the beef cubes in a single layer and cook for 2 to 3 minutes without stirring, until the first side is browned. Turn and brown at least one other side of the cubes. Transfer the beef to a plate.

3. Add the sherry to the Dutch oven and bring to a simmer, scraping the bottom of the pot to get up any browned bits.

4. Stir in the hoisin, rice vinegar, soy sauce, orange juice, ginger, garlic, and red pepper flakes. Add the beef back to the Dutch oven and cover.

5. Place the pot in the oven and cook for 45 minutes to 1 hour, or until the beef is tender. Serve over rice.

TECHNIQUE TIP It's easy to make rice in your Dutch oven, but depending on the size, it can be difficult to make just a small amount. We often make enough for several meals at a time and then reheat it throughout the week. The smallest amount I can make in my large Dutch oven is ½ cup of raw rice, which will yield about 2 cups of cooked rice.

Spicy Beef and Broccoli with Garlic Chips

ACTIVE TIME
30 MINUTES

TOTAL TIME
30 MINUTES

Serves 2

Beef and broccoli is a classic Chinese dish, quick and easy to make at home. The garlic chips are well worth the effort, and yield a complex garlic-scented oil to use in other dishes. You can also use leftover steak to make this dish.

1 (8- to 10-ounce) sirloin or flat iron steak

Kosher salt

¼ cup vegetable oil or more

3 or 4 garlic cloves, peeled and sliced thin

8 to 9 ounces broccoli florets (about 3 cups)

¼ teaspoon red pepper flakes

¼ cup orange juice

¼ cup water

3 tablespoons dry sherry mixed with 2 tablespoons water

3 tablespoons oyster sauce

1. Season the steak with salt on both sides and set aside while you cook the garlic chips.

2. To make the garlic chips, place the Dutch oven over medium heat. Add enough oil to form a layer about ¼-inch deep. Heat until the oil shimmers Add the garlic slices and cook, stirring, for a couple of minutes, until the garlic turns a light brown. Quickly remove the garlic with a large slotted spoon. Drain the garlic chips briefly on a paper towel, then transfer to a small bowl.

3. Pour off all but a thin coating of oil. Save the rest of the oil for other uses. Heat the Dutch oven over medium-high until the oil is shimmering. Add the steak and cook, without moving, for 2 minutes. Turn and cook the other side for 2 minutes. Flip and cook the first side for another minute, then turn and cook the second side for another minute. Transfer the steak to a rack and let it rest for 5 minutes. Cut the steak into ¼-inch slices while the broccoli cooks.

4. If needed, add more oil to form a thin coat at the bottom of the pot. Add the broccoli and red pepper flakes, and sprinkle with salt. Stir to distribute, then add the orange juice and water. Cover and cook for 4 minutes. Remove the lid. The liquid should have evaporated; if not, cook until the liquid is gone.

5. Add the sherry-water mixture and cook until the sherry has mostly evaporated. Add the oyster sauce and steak slices. Turn the heat off and stir to coat with the oyster sauce. Let it sit for a minute or so to heat up the meat.

6. Top with the garlic chips and serve over rice, if desired.

INGREDIENT TIP This dish is also great with shrimp instead of the steak. After cooking the garlic chips, drain off most of the oil, and add 8 to 10 ounces of peeled, deveined shrimp. Sauté for 4 to 5 minutes, or until just done. Add the cooked shrimp back to the pot along with the oyster sauce.

Chicago-Style Italian Beef Sandwiches

ACTIVE TIME
35 MINUTES

TOTAL TIME
2 HOURS
10 MINUTES

Serves 2

I've only tried this Chicago specialty once; it was as delicious as it was messy! A variation on the French dip, the sandwich is traditionally made with sliced roast beef, and topped with green bell peppers and giardiniera (spicy pickled vegetables), then the whole thing is dunked *au jus*. My version uses braised beef rather than sliced roast beef, which is easier to make at home.

2 to 3 tablespoons olive oil

1 small green bell pepper, seeded and cut into bite-size chunks

Kosher salt

¾ pound boneless chuck roast, trimmed of fat

1 small onion, chopped coarsely

1 small carrot, scrubbed or peeled and cut into chunks

2 large garlic cloves, peeled and smashed but left whole

¼ teaspoon peppercorns

1 bay leaf

2 cups water or low-sodium beef stock

2 sturdy hoagie rolls or French rolls

½ cup hot or mild giardiniera, drained

1. Preheat the oven to 300°F.

2. Place the Dutch oven over medium heat. Add enough oil to coat the bottom of the pot and heat until the oil shimmers. Add the bell pepper chunks and cook for 2 to 3 minutes without stirring, so the pieces begin to brown. Stir the peppers and continue to brown, 2 to 3 minutes. The peppers should be blackened in spots and fairly soft. Remove the peppers and set them aside.

3. While the peppers cook, salt the chuck roast. After removing the pepper chunks from the pot, add the roast to the pot and brown for 4 to 5 minutes on one side. Turn and brown at least one other side, then transfer from the pot to a plate or rack.

4. Add the onion to the Dutch oven and cook, stirring, for 2 to 3 minutes, or until the pieces separate and start to soften. Add the carrot and the garlic cloves and cook for another minute or two, or until fragrant and the carrot has begun to soften. Add the peppercorns, bay leaf, water or stock, and ½ teaspoon of salt (if using stock, omit the salt). Bring to a simmer, scraping up the browned bits from the bottom of the pot.

5. Return the roast to the Dutch oven. The liquid should cover the sides of the roast at least halfway; add more liquid if needed.

6. Cook, covered, for 70 to 90 minutes, or until the beef pulls apart with a fork. Remove the roast and place on a rack to cool. Strain the solids from the liquid. If you have a fat separator, pour the sauce in and allow the fat to rise to the surface for 5 to 10 minutes. Pour the sauce back into the pot. If you don't have a fat separator, let the sauce sit for a few minutes to allow the fat to come to the surface of the Dutch oven, and skim or spoon off as much as possible.

7. When the meat is cool enough to handle, slice or break into chunks, discarding any gristle. Return the meat to the liquid. Taste the liquid and adjust the seasoning, adding more salt or pepper if necessary. Add the reserved bell pepper chunks just to warm.

8. Split the rolls almost all the way through, but leave one side attached. Spoon the meat and peppers onto the rolls and drizzle generously with the liquid. Top with the giradiniera and serve with lots of napkins. If you like, pour the remaining liquid into small bowls for dipping.

Mustard-Glazed Short Ribs with Roasted Potatoes

ACTIVE TIME
25 MINUTES

TOTAL TIME
2 HOURS
30 MINUTES

Serves 2

Braising then roasting the short ribs in this recipe results in ultra-tender meat with a tangy, flavorful crust. By roasting the potatoes in the Dutch oven, the result is a one-pot meal.

2 pounds bone-in short ribs

Kosher salt

2 to 3 tablespoons vegetable oil

2 garlic cloves, minced

1 cup beef stock

3 tablespoons Dijon-style mustard

3 tablespoons brown sugar

3 to 4 medium red potatoes, scrubbed and cut into quarters

1 tablespoon olive oil

1. Preheat the oven to 300°F.

2. Season the short ribs on all sides with salt. Place the Dutch oven over medium heat. Add enough oil to coat the bottom of the pot and heat until the oil shimmers. Add the short ribs and cook for 2 to 3 minutes, or until the first side is browned. Turn and brown at least one other side of the ribs. Transfer the ribs to a plate and add the garlic. Cook, stirring, for a minute or so, or until fragrant. Add the beef stock and bring to a simmer, scraping the bottom of the pot to get up the browned bits. Stir in the mustard and brown sugar and simmer until the sugar is dissolved.

3. Add the short ribs back to the Dutch oven. Cook, covered, for about 75 minutes, or until the meat is tender but still attached to the bones.

4. Remove from the oven and turn the heat up to 375°F. Remove the short ribs from the Dutch oven and set them aside.

5. If you have a fat separator, pour the sauce in and allow the fat to rise to the surface for 5 to 10 minutes. Pour the sauce into a small saucepan. If you don't have a fat separator, pour the sauce into a small saucepan and let it sit for a few minutes to allow the fat to come to the surface, and skim off as much as possible. Wipe out the inside of the Dutch oven.

6. Bring the sauce mixture to a boil and cook until it's reduced by about two-thirds, or until it's thick and syrupy, about 15 minutes.

7. Meanwhile, when the Dutch oven has cooled slightly, add the potatoes and olive oil, and toss the potatoes to coat well with the oil, adding more if necessary. Season generously with salt and toss again. Spread the potatoes out into a single layer. Roast, uncovered, for about 15 minutes, or until they are starting to brown.

8. Remove from the oven. Move the potatoes to the perimeter of the Dutch oven and place the short ribs in the center, bone down. (Don't force the potato chunks if they don't move easily; it's okay if the ribs are on top of some of the potatoes.) Brush the glaze over the short ribs and roast for another 15 to 20 minutes, or until the ribs are deeply browned and sticky from the glaze, and the potatoes are browned.

Lamb Shanks and Chickpeas Braised in Garlic Broth

If you've only tried lamb chops or leg of lamb, lamb shanks will be a revelation. Salting them in advance gives them even better flavor and texture, so that they're seasoned throughout and meltingly tender. Chickpeas (garbanzo beans) are a nice accompaniment, and cooking them together saves time and creates a delicious one-pot dinner.

2 large lamb shanks
(about 12 ounces each)

1 teaspoon kosher salt

Freshly ground black pepper

2 to 3 tablespoons olive oil

½ medium onion, chopped
(about ⅔ cup)

4 garlic cloves, sliced thin

1 tablespoon tomato paste

½ cup dry white wine

2½ cups low-sodium chicken stock

¼ pound dried chickpeas, rinsed

1 bay leaf

1 large carrot, peeled and
cut into ½-inch coins

1 tablespoon chopped fresh parsley,
for garnish

1. Season the lamb shanks with the salt and several grinds of pepper. The longer you can do this ahead of time, the better. Cover and let sit for 20 minutes to 2 hours.

2. Preheat the oven to 300°F.

3. Place the Dutch oven over medium heat. Add enough oil to coat the bottom of the pot and heat until the oil shimmers. Add the lamb and sear, turning every 3 to 4 minutes to brown all sides. Remove the lamb and transfer to a plate.

4. Add the onions and garlic and cook, stirring, for 2 to 3 minutes, or until softened but not browned. Add the tomato paste and cook, stirring, until the paste has darkened slightly, about 1 minute. Add the wine and bring to a simmer, scraping to get up any browned bits from the bottom of the Dutch oven.

5. Add the chicken stock, chickpeas, and bay leaf and bring to a simmer. Add the lamb shanks and cover the pot.

6. Place in the oven and bake for 1 hour. Remove the pot from the oven and add the carrot. There should be a visible layer of broth in the Dutch oven; if not, add another ½ cup. Cook, covered, for another 30 to 40 minutes, or until the lamb is almost falling off the bones and the chickpeas are tender.

7. Ladle the lamb, beans, and broth into bowls and garnish with the parsley. Season to taste with additional salt and pepper.

Lamb and White Bean "Cassoulet"

ACTIVE TIME
20 MINUTES

TOTAL TIME
2 ½ TO 3 HOURS

Serves 2

Years ago, then-*LA Times* food writer Russ Parsons published a recipe for what he called "Cowboy Cassoulet," which used lamb instead of duck and sausages. It was written to serve a crowd, and I dutifully followed the recipe exactly. It was delicious, but took all day to put together and cook, and of course I had leftovers for days. I've streamlined his method and changed a few ingredients as well as cutting the quantities to make it manageable for two.

3 tablespoons olive oil, plus more for drizzling

Kosher salt

1 pound lamb shoulder blade chops

1 small carrot, peeled and diced

½ small onion, diced

⅓ cup white wine

⅓ cup crushed tomatoes

1 sprig fresh rosemary left whole, plus 2 teaspoons finely minced leaves

¼ pound dried Great Northern white beans or navy beans

2 cups water or low-sodium chicken stock

Freshly ground black pepper

1 small fennel bulb, trimmed and cut into 4 wedges, core left intact

6 to 8 garlic cloves, peeled but left whole

1 cup fresh bread crumbs (or more depending on the Dutch oven size)

1. Preheat the oven to 300°F.

2. Place the Dutch oven over medium heat. Add enough oil to coat the bottom of the pot and heat until the oil shimmers. While the oil heats, salt the lamb on both sides. Sear the lamb for 3 to 4 minutes or until browned, then turn and sear the other side. Remove the lamb and transfer to a plate.

3. Add the carrot and onion to the Dutch oven and sprinkle with salt. Cook, stirring, for 4 to 5 minutes, or just until the vegetables start to brown. Pour the wine into the pot and stir, scraping up any browned bits from the bottom of the pot. Bring to a boil and reduce by about half.

4. Add the tomatoes, rosemary sprig (reserve the minced leaves for later), beans, water or stock, pepper, and 1 teaspoon of salt. Stir to combine.

5. Lay the fennel pieces and garlic cloves in the pot and push down to submerge in the liquid. Lay the lamb pieces on top and push down to partially submerge.

6. Cover and cook for 1 hour, then remove the pot and check the liquid level. There should still be plenty of liquid covering the beans; if not, pour in another ¼ to ⅓ cup water. Cover the pot and return to the oven. Cook for another hour to 90 minutes, or until the beans and lamb are both very tender.

7. Remove from the oven, and turn the heat up to 400°F.

8. In a small bowl, mix together the bread crumbs, finely minced rosemary, and some black pepper. Sprinkle over the lamb and beans. You should have enough to cover the pot in a layer that mostly covers the contents. Drizzle with olive oil (about a tablespoon, depending on the size of your Dutch oven). Bake uncovered for 15 to 20 more minutes, or until the top is browned.

9. Serve warm.

TECHNIQUE TIP For even better flavor, refrigerate the cooked beans and lamb overnight before adding the crumb topping and browning. Bring to room temperature before finishing, and cook for a little longer to make sure the dish is warmed through.

Greek Lamb Stew

ACTIVE TIME
30 MINUTES

TOTAL TIME
2 HOURS
15 MINUTES

Serves 2

For years, my "go-to" lamb dish was a slow-cooked Middle Eastern lamb curry. It's still one of my favorites, but it does require an overnight marinade and a very well-stocked spice cabinet. This Greek-influenced stew is less labor intensive and requires fewer ingredients. The lemon and herbs brighten the flavor, so don't skip using them.

1 pound boneless lamb shoulder, trimmed of fat and cut into 2-inch pieces

Kosher salt

2 to 3 tablespoons olive oil

1 small onion, diced

2 large garlic cloves, minced

1 tablespoon tomato paste

½ cup white wine

1 cup low-sodium chicken stock

1 large tomato, seeded and chopped (or use about ⅔ cup diced canned tomatoes)

1 celery stalk, cut into ¼-inch pieces

1 sprig rosemary

1 bay leaf

½ lemon, juiced (about 1 tablespoon), plus ½ teaspoon lemon zest

2 teaspoons chopped fresh mint

2 tablespoons chopped fresh parsley

1. Preheat the oven to 325°F. Season the lamb liberally with salt on all sides.

2. Place the Dutch oven over medium heat. Add enough oil to coat the bottom of the pot and heat until the oil shimmers. Add half the lamb pieces in a single layer and cook for 2 to 3 minutes without stirring, until the first side is browned. Turn and brown at least one other side of the cubes. Transfer the lamb to a plate and repeat with the remaining lamb pieces.

3. Add the onion and garlic to the Dutch oven, stirring, for 2 to 3 minutes, or until the onion is beginning to soften and separate. Add the tomato paste and stir, breaking it up as much as possible. Cook for 2 to 3 minutes, or until it has darkened slightly.

4. Add the wine and bring to a boil, scraping to release the browned bits from the bottom of the pan. Reduce the wine by about half, and add the chicken stock, tomato, celery, rosemary, and bay leaf and bring to a simmer. Add the lamb back to the Dutch oven and cover.

5. Cook for 75 to 90 minutes, or until the lamb is very tender. Take the lamb out of the Dutch oven and place on a rack to cool. If you have a fat separator, strain the solids from the liquid and pour the sauce into the separator. Allow the fat to rise to the surface for 5 to 10 minutes and pour the sauce and the solids back into the pot. If you don't have a fat separator, let the sauce sit for a few minutes to allow the fat to come to the surface of the Dutch oven, and skim or spoon off as much as possible.

6. Stir in the lemon juice and zest and taste the sauce, adjusting the seasoning as necessary. Bring to a simmer and add the lamb to reheat. Stir in the mint and parsley and serve.

INGREDIENT TIP If you get to know the people in your meat department, you can sometimes have them cut up a chunk of lamb shoulder (or boneless leg, which will also work) for you, which is a big time-saver.

BREADS & DESSERTS

chapter eight

Parmesan-Garlic Pull-Apart Rolls

ACTIVE TIME
30 MINUTES

TOTAL TIME
55 MINUTES
PLUS RISING TIME

SMALL SIZE
(HALF-BATCH)
**makes 3 to
4 servings**

LARGE SIZE
(FULL BATCH)
**makes 6 to
8 servings**

VEGETARIAN

Nothing beats fresh bread. The dough for these rolls (also used in the Cinnamon-Raisin Pull-Apart Rolls, page 190) is enough for a large Dutch oven; use half the dough if you have a small (2- to 3.5-quart) pot. You can freeze or refrigerate whatever you don't use.

For assembly, use the first ingredient amounts for the half batch and the amounts in parentheses for the full batch.

FOR THE DOUGH

1 cup milk

⅓ cup water

2 tablespoons unsalted butter (at room temperature)

2 tablespoons granulated sugar

1 package (¼-ounce) rapid rise, instant, or active dry yeast

3¼ cups all-purpose flour, plus extra for work surface

2 teaspoons fine salt

Cooking spray or vegetable oil

FOR THE ASSEMBLY

4 (8) tablespoons unsalted butter, cut into 1-tablespoon pieces

1 (2) large garlic cloves, minced or pressed

1½ (3) cups finely shredded Parmigiano-Reggiano cheese

1. For the dough, in a 2-cup (or larger) glass or microwave-safe measuring cup, add the milk, water, and butter. Heat the mixture in the microwave to about 110°F/46°C. If the butter is soft to begin with, it melts by the time the milk is warm. Then whisk in the sugar and yeast. Let the mixture sit for 5 to 7 minutes or until the yeast is foaming.

2. If you have a stand mixer, add the flour and salt in the bowl and mix briefly with the paddle to distribute the salt evenly. Turn the machine to low and slowly add the milk mixture.

3. After the dough comes together, switch to the dough hook. Increase the speed to medium and mix until the dough holds together in a ball, 4 to 7 minutes. The dough should be sticky; if it's too wet to hold together, add a little more flour. Turn it onto a lightly floured surface and knead briefly to form a smooth, round ball. It should be stickier and softer than typical bread dough.

4. To mix by hand, whisk together the flour and salt in a large mixing bowl. Add the wet ingredients and stir until the dough holds together. Turn out onto a lightly floured board and knead for 5 to 9 minutes, or until you have a smooth, round ball.

5. Coat the bottom and sides of a large bowl with cooking spray or a thin layer of vegetable oil. Place the dough in the bowl and coat the surface with more cooking spray or oil. Cover the bowl with plastic wrap and place in a warm place until the dough doubles in size, about 1 hour.

6. Lightly punch down the dough. If you are using a small Dutch oven (2- to 3.5-quart), divide the dough and freeze half of it. If you are using a larger Dutch oven, use the whole batch.

7. To assemble, place the butter in a microwave-safe bowl and add the garlic. Microwave on half-power for about a minute, or just until melted, stirring halfway through. Using a pastry brush, lightly coat the bottom and sides of the Dutch oven with a little of the butter.

8. Pour the cheese into a shallow bowl. »

9. Divide the dough into small balls about 1-inch in diameter. (I use a small ice cream scoop for this, but you can also just pinch off pieces of dough. You can also cut the dough all at once with a bench scraper. If so, spread the dough pieces out on a sheet of parchment paper so they're not touching; they're sticky and have a tendency to clump together.)

10. A few at a time, place the dough pieces in the melted butter and roll around to coat thoroughly. Transfer to the cheese and roll to coat lightly. You may find a small slotted spoon or two forks to be helpful. Place the cheese-coated dough balls in the prepared Dutch oven. They should be touching but not crowded. Repeat with the remaining dough balls, spacing them evenly in 2 to 3 layers (depending on the size of your Dutch oven). Drizzle with the remaining butter and sprinkle with any remaining cheese.

11. Cover the pan lightly with a piece of plastic wrap. Set the pan in a warm place and let rise until almost doubled, about 50 to 60 minutes.

12. Toward the end of the dough's rising time, preheat the oven to 350°F.

13. Bake, uncovered, for 20 to 25 minutes, or until the top is puffed up and browned.

14. Let the rolls cool in the Dutch oven for about 15 minutes, then carefully unmold. Let cool for another 5 minutes or so before serving.

TECHNIQUE TIP The rolls can be frozen for up to a month. Let cool completely, then wrap tightly in foil and seal in a plastic bag. To serve, let thaw at room temperature for 30 minutes or so; reheat for 15 to 20 minutes in a 200°F oven.

Quick Biscuits

Two-ingredient biscuits are a godsend. Award-winning cookbook authors, including Kenji Lopez-Alt of Serious Eats and Southerner Nathalie Dupree, both agree, it yields terrific biscuits with very little effort.

4 ounces self-rising flour (just under 1 cup), plus a little more for dusting

4 ounces heavy cream (½ cup)

ACTIVE TIME
10 MINUTES

TOTAL TIME
20 MINUTES

Makes 4 large or 6 small biscuits

VEGETARIAN

1. Preheat the oven to 450°F. Lightly grease the Dutch oven on the bottom and 2 inches up the sides.

2. In a medium bowl, add the flour and drizzle the cream over it. Stir until combined.

3. Dust a little more flour over a cutting board and transfer the dough to the board. Knead it briefly until it forms a fairly smooth ball; flatten it out into a rectangle about ½-inch thick. Fold one end to the middle of the dough and the other end over it, so the dough is in three layers. Flatten it out again until it's about ½-inch thick (you can use a rolling pin for this; I usually just do it by hand).

4. Use a biscuit cutter or glass to form as many biscuits as possible, rerolling the scraps once only.

5. Place the biscuits in the prepared Dutch oven so that they touch on the sides (if the biscuits are touching, they will rise slightly higher than if separated).

6. Bake for 10 to 12 minutes, or until golden brown. Remove from the oven and let cool for a few minutes before serving.

TECHNIQUE TIP If you have a kitchen scale, this recipe is really easy to scale; if you measure equal amounts by weight of self-rising flour and cream, you can't go wrong.

No-Knead Bread

ACTIVE TIME
15 MINUTES

TOTAL TIME
75 MINUTES
PLUS RISING TIME

**Makes
1 loaf,
about
1½ pounds**

VEGAN

This is my version of Mark Bittman's version of Jim Lahey's original no-knead bread recipe. It makes a broad, open-crumbed loaf with a very crisp crust. Many people are confused by how little yeast is called for—a mere ¼ teaspoon—because the typical bread recipe uses ¼ ounce (the amount in a standard envelope of yeast). The long rise gives the yeast plenty of time to multiply; that same slow rise accounts for the bread's complex flavor.

3 cups (450 grams) all-purpose flour

¼ teaspoon (1 gram) active dry yeast

1½ teaspoons (9 grams) fine salt

1⅝ cups (385 grams) water

Cooking spray or vegetable oil

1. In a large bowl, combine the flour, yeast, and salt. Add the water and stir until thoroughly blended. The dough will look loose and sticky. Cover the bowl with plastic wrap and set in a warm spot for 12 to 18 hours (the longer the better).

2. Lightly flour a clean counter or cutting board.

3. After the first rise, the dough should be covered with bubbles, and it will have grown considerably in size. Turn it out onto your floured surface; flour your fingers. Using your hands and/or a dough scraper, fold the dough onto itself a few times to deflate it. Cover it (right on the board) with plastic wrap and let it sit for 15 minutes.

4. Meanwhile, coat another large bowl with cooking spray or oil. Using just enough flour to keep the dough from sticking to your fingers or the board, work the dough into a rough ball, and place it in the prepared bowl.

5. Cover the bowl with a clean kitchen towel and let it rise until doubled, about 2 hours. It should not spring back when you poke it, although it will still be sticky.

6. Ninety minutes into the second rise, preheat the oven to 450°F. Put your Dutch oven—lid and all—to heat in the oven.

7. When the dough is ready, carefully turn the dough out of the bowl and into the hot Dutch oven. Give the pot a shake to distribute the dough across the bottom of the pot, but don't worry too much about how the top of the dough looks; most irregularities will level out during baking.

8. Bake, covered, for 30 minutes. Then remove the lid and bake for another 20 to 30 minutes, until the loaf is browned.

9. Remove the pot from the oven and turn the loaf out onto a cooling rack.

TECHNIQUE TIP If you use a 5-quart Dutch oven, you'll end up with a relatively flat loaf, something akin to ciabatta. A smaller Dutch oven will yield a taller loaf and you may need to increase the baking time.

Olive Herb Bread

ACTIVE TIME
15 MINUTES

TOTAL TIME
75 MINUTES
PLUS RISING TIME

**Makes
1 loaf,
about
1½ pounds**

VEGAN

This bread is a variation on No-Knead Bread (page 182). Head to your supermarket's olive bar to buy a pleasing mix of green and black olives. I love the combination of olives and rosemary, but thyme and oregano are also good choices.

3 cups (450 grams) all-purpose flour

¼ teaspoon (1 gram) active dry yeast

1½ teaspoons (9 grams) fine salt

1⅝ cups (385 grams) water

Cooking spray or vegetable oil

¾ cup mixed green and black pitted olives, coarsely chopped

2 tablespoons minced fresh rosemary, thyme, or oregano (or a combination)

1. In a large bowl, combine the flour, yeast, and salt. Add the water and stir until thoroughly blended. The dough will look loose and sticky. Cover the bowl with plastic wrap and set in a warm spot for 12 to 18 hours (the longer the better).

2. Lightly flour a clean counter or cutting board.

3. After the first rise, the dough should be covered with bubbles, and it will have grown considerably in size. Turn it out onto a floured surface; flour your fingers. Using your hands and/or a dough scraper, fold the dough onto itself a few times to deflate it. Cover it (right on the board) with plastic wrap and let it sit for 15 minutes.

4. Meanwhile, coat another large bowl with cooking spray or oil. Using just enough flour to keep the dough from sticking to your fingers or the board, work the chopped olives and herbs into the dough. Then work the dough into a rough ball, and place it in the prepared bowl.

5. Cover the bowl with a clean kitchen towel and let it rise until doubled, about 2 hours. It should not spring back when you poke it, although it will still be sticky.

6. Ninety minutes into the second rise, preheat the oven to 450°F. Put your Dutch oven—lid and all—to heat in the oven.

7. When the dough is ready, carefully turn the dough out of the bowl and into the hot Dutch oven. Give the pot a shake to distribute the dough across the bottom of the pot, but don't worry too much about how the top of the dough looks; most irregularities will level out during baking.

8. Bake, covered, for 30 minutes. Then remove the lid and bake for another 20 to 30 minutes, until the loaf is browned.

9. Remove the pot from the oven and turn the loaf out onto a cooling rack.

Bacon-Cheddar Biscuits

ACTIVE TIME
30 MINUTES

TOTAL TIME
50 MINUTES

**Makes
4 large or
6 small
biscuits**

It might not seem possible to improve on Quick Biscuits (page 181), but adding cheese, bacon, and chives is a great way to do exactly that. These hearty biscuits go particularly well with soups, stews, or salads. They're also great for breakfast, alone or with eggs.

2 thick or 3 thin slices bacon

1¼ cups all-purpose flour

¼ teaspoon fine salt

2 teaspoons baking powder

¼ teaspoon cream of tartar

¼ teaspoon sugar

1 to 2 tablespoons butter, chilled

2 ounces sharp Cheddar cheese, grated (about ½ cup)

1 tablespoon minced fresh chives

¼ cup very cold whole milk, or more as needed

1 tablespoon plain whole-milk yogurt

2 teaspoons melted butter for finishing (optional)

1. Preheat the oven to 450°F. Lightly grease the Dutch oven on the bottom and 2 inches up the sides.

2. In a small skillet, fry the bacon until crisp and most of the fat has rendered. Remove the bacon slices and drain on paper towels. Pour the accumulated bacon fat through a fine strainer into a small bowl and measure it. You should have 1 or 2 tablespoons; if you have more than 3, discard any extra or save it for another use. Return the fat to the small bowl and refrigerate or freeze it until very firm. Chop the bacon and set it aside. You should have about ¼ cup.

3. In a small bowl, sift or whisk together the flour, salt, baking powder, cream of tartar, and sugar. Sifting the dry ingredients makes for lighter, fluffier biscuits; if you don't sift, make sure to whisk thoroughly to combine.

4. Measure enough chilled butter so that when added to the reserved chilled bacon fat, you have 3 tablespoons. Cut it into small cubes. Cut the chilled bacon fat into small pieces.

5. Using a fork, a pastry blender, or your fingers, cut the butter and bacon fat into the flour mixture until you have only small pieces of fat remaining. Stir in the cheese, chopped bacon, and chives. Note: You can make the biscuit mixture ahead to this point. Refrigerate until ready to continue.

6. When you're ready to form and bake the biscuits, whisk together the milk and yogurt, add it to the dry ingredients, and stir just until the dough holds together. If the dough is too dry, add a little more milk, a teaspoon at a time. The dough should be a bit sticky, but not wet.

7. On a lightly floured surface, pat the dough into an oval about ½-inch thick. Cut into 4 large or 6 small biscuits (depending on size) with a biscuit cutter or knife. If necessary, roll the scraps together to cut the last biscuit or two, but try not to handle the dough too much.

8. Place the biscuits in the prepared Dutch oven so that they touch on the sides (if the biscuits are touching, they will rise slightly higher than if separated).

9. Bake for 10 to 12 minutes, or until golden brown. If you like, brush the tops of the biscuits with the optional melted butter. Serve warm.

INGREDIENT TIP If you don't have fresh chives, you can substitute fresh chopped parsley or the green part of a scallion, finely minced. If you don't have either of those, just leave them out. I don't suggest using dried chives, as they impart very little flavor.

Garlic Naan

Traditionally, the Indian bread called *naan* is made in a *tandoor*, a clay oven that is intensely hot. I make no claim to authenticity with my Dutch oven version, but there's no denying that it's delicious. Infusing the oil with garlic takes a little time, but adds tons of flavor.

3 tablespoons vegetable oil

3 large garlic cloves, two smashed and one minced

1 teaspoon active dry yeast

2 teaspoons sugar

½ cup warm water (about 110°F)

2 cups all-purpose flour, plus more as needed

1 teaspoon fine sea salt

¼ teaspoon baking powder

3 tablespoons plain yogurt

1 tablespoon milk

Vegetable oil

3 tablespoons butter

Kosher salt, for sprinkling

1. Place the Dutch oven over medium heat and add the oil. When it shimmers, add the two smashed cloves of garlic and cook for 5 to 6 minutes, or until the garlic is golden brown. Pour off all the oil but leave a light coating and turn off the heat. Discard the garlic and measure 2 tablespoons of the oil and set aside. Let it cool.

2. In a small bowl, combine the yeast, sugar, and warm water. Let stand until foamy, 5 to 10 minutes.

3. Place the flour, salt, and baking powder in the bowl of a stand mixer with the paddle attachment. Mix to blend. Add the yeast mixture, yogurt, milk, and the 2 tablespoons of garlic oil, and mix to combine. Switch to the dough hook and beat until smooth and elastic, 5 to 8 minutes. The dough should be soft but not too sticky. Add flour as needed.

4. To mix by hand, whisk together the flour, salt, and baking powder in a large mixing bowl. Add the wet ingredients and stir until the dough holds together. Turn out onto a lightly floured surface and knead for 5 to 9 minutes, or until you have a smooth round ball.

5. Place the dough in a large, lightly oiled bowl, turning to coat all sides. Cover the bowl with plastic wrap, then a kitchen towel. Let the dough rise in a warm, draft-free spot until doubled, 1 to 1½ hours.

6. Punch down the dough and divide into 4 to 6 equal pieces. Roll them into balls, place them on a lightly floured baking sheet and cover with a slightly damp kitchen towel. Let them rise until doubled in size, 40 to 60 minutes.

7. Place the Dutch oven (still with the light coating of garlic oil) over medium heat while you roll the naan. The Dutch oven should be very hot, but the oil should not be smoking. Have the lid nearby.

8. Add the minced garlic to the butter in a small microwaveable bowl and heat until melted and fragrant. Keep the butter and a basting brush near the Dutch oven.

9. On a lightly floured surface, roll out the dough balls to about ¼-inch thick. Traditionally, naan are shaped like a teardrop; if you like, as you pick up the naans to cook, let the weight of the dough pull the circles into the shape of a teardrop.

10. Gently lay one of the pieces of naan in the Dutch oven. The dough should start to bubble. Cook for 1 minute; flip the naan. It should be blistered and somewhat blackened in places. Cover the skillet with the lid and cook 30 seconds to 1 minute more, or until puffy and browned on the second side.

11. Remove the naan from the Dutch oven, brush with a bit of garlic butter, and sprinkle with kosher salt. Place the naan in a towel-lined dish and cover with the towel to keep warm. Repeat with the rest of the naans and serve.

INGREDIENT TIP If you have leftover oil from frying the garlic chips for Spicy Beef and Broccoli (page 164), you can use that in this recipe.

Cinnamon-Raisin Pull-Apart Bread

ACTIVE TIME
30 MINUTES

TOTAL TIME
55 MINUTES
PLUS RISING TIME

SMALL SIZE
(HALF-BATCH)
**makes 3 to
4 servings**

LARGE SIZE
(FULL BATCH)
**makes 6 to
8 servings**

VEGETARIAN

This tastes very much like Monkey Bread but in a slightly different form with raisins added. The amount of dough is enough for a large Dutch oven; use half the dough if you have a small (2- to 3.5-quart) one (the rest can be frozen or refrigerated).

For assembly, use the first ingredient amounts for the half batch and the amounts in parentheses for the full batch.

FOR THE DOUGH

1 cup milk

⅓ cup water

2 tablespoons unsalted butter

2 tablespoons granulated sugar

1 package (¼-ounce) rapid rise, instant, or active dry yeast

3¼ cups all-purpose flour, plus extra for work surface

2 teaspoons fine salt

Cooking spray or vegetable oil

FOR THE ASSEMBLY

4 (8) tablespoons unsalted butter, melted

½ (1) cup firmly packed light or dark brown sugar

1 (2) teaspoon ground cinnamon (or more)

¼ (½) cup raisins

1. In a 2-cup (or larger) glass or microwave-safe measuring cup, add the milk, water, and butter. Heat the mixture in the microwave to about 110°F/46°C. If the butter is soft to begin with, it melts by the time the milk is warm. Then whisk in the sugar and yeast. Let the mixture sit for 5 to 7 minutes or until the yeast is foaming.

2. If you have a stand mixer, add the flour and salt to the bowl and mix briefly with the paddle to distribute the salt evenly. Turn the machine to low and slowly add the milk mixture. After the dough comes together, switch to the dough hook. Increase the speed to medium and mix until the dough holds together in a ball, 4 to 7 minutes. The dough should be sticky; if it's too wet to hold together, add a little more flour. Turn it onto a lightly floured surface and knead briefly to form a smooth, round ball. It should be stickier and softer than typical bread dough.

3. To mix by hand, whisk together the flour and salt in a large mixing bowl. Add the wet ingredients and stir until the dough holds together. Turn out onto a lightly floured surface and knead for 5 to 9 minutes, or until you have a smooth round ball.

4. Coat the bottom and sides of a large bowl with cooking spray or a thin layer of vegetable oil. Place the dough in the bowl and coat the surface with more cooking spray or oil. Cover the bowl with plastic wrap and place in a warm place until the dough doubles in size, about an hour.

5. Lightly punch down the dough. If you are using a small Dutch oven (2- to 3.5-quart), divide the dough and freeze half of it. If you are using a larger Dutch oven, use the whole batch. You'll have leftovers, which can be wrapped in aluminum foil and frozen.

6. For the assembly, pour the melted butter into a small bowl. Using a pastry brush, lightly coat the bottom and sides of the Dutch oven with a little of the butter.

7. In a shallow bowl, stir together the brown sugar and cinnamon.

8. Divide the dough into small balls about 1 inch in diameter. (I use a small ice cream scoop for this, but you can also just pinch off pieces of dough. You can also cut the dough all at once with a bench scraper. If so, spread the dough pieces out on a sheet of parchment paper so they're not touching; they're sticky and have a tendency to clump together.) »

9. A few at a time, place the dough pieces in the melted butter and roll around to coat thoroughly. Transfer to the cinnamon-sugar mixture and roll to coat. You may find a small slotted spoon or two forks to be helpful. Place the sugar-coated dough balls in the prepared Dutch oven. They should be touching but not crowded. As you place 5 or 6 of the balls in the pot, sprinkle with some of the raisins, pushing them down in between the balls. Repeat with the remaining dough balls and raisins, spacing them evenly in 2 to 3 layers (depending on the size of your Dutch oven). Drizzle with the remaining butter and sprinkle with a little additional sugar to coat evenly.

10. Cover the pan lightly with a piece of plastic wrap. Set the pan in a warm place and let it rise until almost doubled, about 50 to 60 minutes.

11. After 20 to 30 minutes, preheat the oven to 350°F.

12. Bake, uncovered, for 20 to 25 minutes, or until the top is puffed up and browned and you see some sugar syrup bubbling around the edges.

13. Let the bread cool in the Dutch oven for about 15 minutes, then carefully unmold. Let cool for another 5 minutes or so before serving.

TECHNIQUE TIP While this bread is best served warm, it can also be frozen for up to a month. Let cool completely, then place uncovered in the freezer so the syrup sets up. Then, wrap tightly in foil and seal in a plastic bag. To serve, let thaw at room temperature for 30 minutes or so. To reheat, wrap loosely in foil, and heat at 250°F/120°C for 15 minutes.

One-Pan Fudgy Brownies

I usually mix these brownies in a bowl and then pour them into a buttered pan, but they also work when mixed and baked in a Dutch oven, and it's certainly easier that way. You'll want to melt the chocolate and butter slowly, over the lowest heat possible, so that the Dutch oven doesn't get so hot that it cooks the eggs.

As with other desserts, the first amounts will work in a 2- to 3.5-quart Dutch oven and the amounts in parentheses will work in one up to 5 quarts.

ACTIVE TIME
15 MINUTES

TOTAL TIME
40 MINUTES

SMALL SIZE
makes 3 to 4 servings

LARGE SIZE
makes 6 to 8 servings

VEGETARIAN

4 (8) tablespoons unsalted butter

4 (8) ounces dark chocolate (65 to 72 percent cacao)

½ (1) cup sugar

1 (2) teaspoon vanilla extract

Pinch salt

1 (2) egg

6 tablespoons (¾ cup) flour

1. Preheat the oven to 350°F.

2. Place the Dutch oven over low heat, and melt the butter and chocolate, stirring, until melted. Remove from the heat and let it cool slightly.

3. Stir in the sugar, vanilla, and salt. Add the egg(s), one at a time, and stir until blended. Add the flour to the chocolate mixture and beat until smooth, about a minute.

4. Smooth out the batter into the bottom of the Dutch oven, and use a damp paper towel to wipe off any batter from the sides of the pot (it will burn).

5. Bake, uncovered, for 20 to 30 minutes, or until a toothpick inserted into the center comes out with crumbs sticking to it but no raw batter. Let it cool for 10 minutes or so. Use a silicone-coated spatula to cut the brownies into wedges and remove them from the Dutch oven.

Blackberry Cobbler

ACTIVE TIME
20 MINUTES

TOTAL TIME
50 MINUTES

SMALL SIZE
**makes 3 to
4 servings**

LARGE SIZE
**makes 6 to
8 servings**

VEGETARIAN

Cobblers, fruit desserts topped with sweet biscuit-like dough, are tremendously flexible, and can be made in many different pot sizes. If you have a small (2- to 3.5-quart) Dutch oven, use the first amount of filling ingredients; if you have a larger one, use the amounts in parentheses. The amount of topping is almost too much for a very small Dutch oven, and for a very large oven, it might not be quite as much as is ideal, but it's very adaptable.

Butter, for greasing the pot

FOR THE FILLING
3½ (6) cups fresh blackberries

2 tablespoons (¼ cup) cornstarch

½ (1) cup granulated sugar

FOR THE TOPPING
¾ cup self-rising flour

2 tablespoons granulated sugar

¼ teaspoon ground cinnamon

½ cup heavy cream, or more
as needed

1 tablespoon melted butter

FOR THE ASSEMBLY
1 tablespoon heavy cream

2 tablespoons granulated sugar

1. Preheat the oven to 350°F. Generously butter the bottom of the Dutch oven and up about 2 inches on the sides.

2. For the filling, mix together the blackberries, cornstarch, and sugar. Pour into the prepared Dutch oven.

3. For the topping, whisk together the flour, sugar, and cinnamon. In a separate bowl, whisk together the cream and butter. Add to the dry ingredients and stir just until combined. If the mixture is too dry to come together, add more cream, a teaspoon at a time, until the dough holds together in a ball but is very sticky.

4. Using two spoons, scoop out 2 to 3 tablespoons of dough and place it over the fruit in the center of the Dutch oven. Scoop out the rest in similar-sized pieces and arrange evenly over the top of the fruit. In a small Dutch oven, you won't see much fruit through the topping; in a larger pot, you'll see more. As much as possible, smooth out the dough and spread it slightly. (I prefer a smoother top so the dough browns more evenly.) Brush the topping with the cream and sprinkle with sugar.

5. Bake, uncovered, for 20 to 25 minutes, or until the topping is browned and the fruit is bubbling. Remove from the oven and let cool for 10 minutes before serving.

Peach and Blueberry Crisp

ACTIVE TIME
20 MINUTES

TOTAL TIME
50 MINUTES

SMALL SIZE
**makes 3 to
4 servings**

LARGE SIZE
**makes 6 to
8 servings**

VEGETARIAN

This is the first dessert we have our beginning cooking students prepare; it's easy and very forgiving. You can use pears or plums instead of the peaches with equally delicious results; if the fruit is not completely ripe, you may have to cook the crisp longer. If you have a 2- to 3-quart Dutch oven, use the first amounts of ingredients; you'll have two very generous servings or four moderate ones. If you're using a 4.5- to 5.5-quart pot, use the amounts in parentheses. You'll have lots of leftovers, which can be refrigerated.

FOR THE CRISP

Butter, for greasing the pot

3 (6) large ripe peaches

¾ (1½) cup frozen blueberries, thawed and drained

½ (1) cup granulated sugar

1 (2) tablespoon cornstarch

¼ (½) teaspoon grated lemon zest

FOR THE TOPPING

⅓ (⅔) cup quick-cooking oatmeal

¼ (½) cup (packed) brown sugar

¼ (½) cup all-purpose flour

2 tablespoons (¼ cup) blanched slivered almonds

⅛ (¼) teaspoon ground cardamom

½ (1) teaspoon ground cinnamon

Pinch kosher salt

3 (6) tablespoons unsalted butter, plus more for buttering baking dishes

1. Preheat the oven to 350° F.

2. Generously butter the bottom of the Dutch oven and up about 2 inches on the sides.

3. For the crisp, peel and slice the peaches into ¼-inch pieces. In a medium bowl, add the peaches and blueberries along with the sugar, cornstarch, and lemon zest. Toss gently. Pour into the prepared Dutch oven.

4. For the topping, mix together the oatmeal, brown sugar, flour, almonds, cardamom, cinnamon, and salt in a medium bowl. With a pastry cutter or a large fork, cut in the butter until the mixture is crumbly. You can do this in a food processor if you have one, but don't overprocess since you want a crumbly texture. Sprinkle the topping evenly over the fruit. Bake for 30 minutes, or until the top is lightly browned and the peaches are bubbling.

TECHNIQUE TIP Crisp is best served warm, and wonderful topped with ice cream. If you have leftovers, heat them in a low oven for 15 minutes or so.

Mixed Fruit Galette

ACTIVE TIME
15 MINUTES

TOTAL TIME
40 MINUTES

Makes 2 to 4 servings

VEGETARIAN

A galette is a free-form pie or tart. It's less fussy and time consuming than either tarts or pies, and this one is even easier because it uses any combination of frozen fruit you like. Using the bottom of a Dutch oven as a baking stone yields a crisp galette with a perfectly browned bottom.

FOR THE CRUST

4¼ ounces flour (about 1 cup)

3 ounces butter (6 tablespoons), chilled, cut into small cubes

⅛ teaspoon kosher salt

⅛ teaspoon sugar

2 tablespoons ice cold water

FOR THE FILLING

1 generous cup mixed frozen fruit, thawed

¼ cup granulated sugar

1 tablespoon cornstarch

FOR THE ASSEMBLY

1 egg, separated

1 teaspoon cream or milk

2 tablespoons coarse "sanding" sugar or granulated sugar

1. For the crust, add the flour, butter, salt, and sugar in the bowl of a small food processor. Process on pulse until the fat is cut uniformly into the flour in very small pieces. Add the water all at once, and process just until the dough holds together. If the dough is too dry to stick together, add more water in teaspoon increments.

2. If you don't have a food processor, mix together the flour, sugar, and salt. Cut in the butter with a pastry blender or large heavy fork until the flour mixture is in small pieces. Stir in the water to form a rough ball.

3. Transfer the dough, which may be slightly crumbly, to a large sealable plastic bag. Seal it, and use the palm of your hand to knead the dough once or twice until it forms a smooth disk. Refrigerate for 20 minutes while you prepare the filling.

4. For the filling, drain the fruit and reserve about a tablespoon of the juice in a small bowl. In a medium bowl, combine the fruit and the sugar, stirring to dissolve. Whisk the cornstarch into the reserved fruit juice and add to the fruit in the bowl. Stir to combine.

5. Preheat the oven to 375°F. Place the Dutch oven, upside down, on the lowest rack. If you like, place it on top of a piece of aluminum foil or a large sheet pan in case the galette drips.

6. Take a piece of parchment paper and, using the bottom of the Dutch oven as a guide, trace a circle (a Sharpie works well for this). Turn the parchment paper over so the ink is on the underside. Place the disk of dough on the parchment and use your hand to flatten it out to about ¾-inch thick. Cover with another piece of parchment paper and roll the dough out to the size of the circle; don't worry if it's a bit misshapen. Remove the top piece of parchment paper but leave the dough on the bottom piece.

7. For the assembly, lightly beat the egg white. Brush the dough up to about 1 inch from the edges, with the egg white. Spoon the fruit in the center of the dough, leaving at least a 1½-inch border. Fold the dough edges over the filling, pleating it to form an attractive border.

8. Whisk the egg yolk with the cream or milk and brush over the border of the crust. Sprinkle both the crust and the fruit with the sugar. Leaving the galette on the parchment paper, use a pizza peel or rimless cookie sheet to transfer the galette to the bottom surface of the Dutch oven. Bake for 18 to 20 minutes, or until the fruit is bubbling and the crust is browned.

9. Again, using the pizza peel or cookie sheet, remove the galette from the oven (don't try to move the Dutch oven itself). Place the galette, parchment paper and all, on a rack to cool. When the oven has cooled, carefully remove the Dutch oven and place it on the stove top to cool completely.

Creamy Lemon Cheesecakes

ACTIVE TIME
15 MINUTES

TOTAL TIME
40 MINUTES
PLUS
CHILLING TIME

**Makes
4 small
cheesecakes**

VEGETARIAN

Baking four small cheesecakes goes much faster than one large dessert, so you'll be able to enjoy these individual treats in less time. Sweet and tangy, they call for limoncello, which is an Italian lemon liqueur. If you don't have limoncello, just use brandy.

FOR THE CRUST

⅔ cup vanilla wafer cookie crumbs or graham cracker crumbs

3 tablespoons butter, melted, plus additional butter for coating the ramekins

FOR THE FILLING

2 tablespoons sour cream

6 ounces cream cheese, softened

¼ cup granulated sugar

1 large egg

1 teaspoon grated lemon zest

1 teaspoon freshly squeezed lemon juice

2 teaspoons limoncello or brandy

½ teaspoon vanilla extract

1. Preheat the oven to 300°F.

2. Set four empty ramekins or custard cups in the Dutch oven and add enough water to come up to within ½ inch of the tops of the ramekins. Remove the ramekins and heat the water over medium-high heat just until simmering.

3. While the water heats, prepare the crust. Mix the cookie crumbs with the butter. Brush the insides with softened butter to make removal easier. Scoop out about 2 tablespoons of the crumb mixture into each of the ramekins. For a crisper crust, place the ramekins in the oven and bake for 5 to 8 minutes or until lightly browned and fragrant. Let the ramekins cool.

4. For the filling, in a small bowl add the sour cream and cream cheese and beat until smooth with a hand mixer. Add the sugar gradually, continuing to beat until the mixture is smooth again. Beat in the egg until fully incorporated. Mix in the lemon zest, lemon juice, liqueur, and vanilla.

5. Divide the cheesecake batter between the ramekins (a generous ¼ cup is about the right amount).

6. When the water in the Dutch oven is just barely simmering, move the pot into the oven. Pull out the oven rack and, using tongs, place the ramekins in the simmering water. Bake the cheesecakes for 25 to 30 minutes, or until barely set. Carefully remove the Dutch oven and then, using tongs, remove the ramekins from the water. Let cool for 5 to 10 minutes, then place the ramekins on a small sheet pan or plate and refrigerate to chill thoroughly (3 hours to overnight).

Coffee Pots de Crème

ACTIVE TIME
15 MINUTES

TOTAL TIME
55 MINUTES
PLUS CHILLING
TIME

**Makes
4 small
custards**

VEGETARIAN

Pots de crème, literally pots of cream or custard, are rich-baked custards. They are traditionally prepared in small pots with lids, which keep a skin from forming on top, or you can use ramekins.

¾ cup whole milk

¾ cup heavy cream

2 tablespoons instant
espresso powder

4 egg yolks

½ cup sugar

1. Preheat the oven to 325°F.

2. Set four empty 1-cup custard cups or ramekins in the Dutch oven and add enough water to the pot to come up to within ½ inch of the tops of the ramekins. Remove the ramekins and heat the water over medium-high heat just until simmering. As soon as the water reaches a simmer, turn off the heat and place the pot in the oven.

3. While the water heats, add the milk and cream to a 2-cup glass or microwave-safe measuring cup and stir in the espresso powder. In the microwave, heat just to a simmer (or heat in a saucepan on the stove). While the milk heats, add the egg yolks and sugar to a small bowl and whisk for about 2 minutes or until the mixture turns slightly pale. Slowly pour in the milk-cream mixture until the mixture is homogeneous; no streaks of egg should remain. Strain the mixture through a small sieve into the ramekins, and cover each one with a square of aluminum foil.

4. Pull out the oven rack and carefully place the ramekins in the Dutch oven. Bake the custards for 35 to 40 minutes with the lid off of the Dutch oven, or until the custard is set (remove the foil and gently wiggle one to check; the center should not be liquid).

5. Carefully remove the Dutch oven and then, using tongs, remove the ramekins from the water. Let cool for 25 to 30 minutes, then refrigerate for at least 2 hours to set. Serve with whipped cream, if desired.

Spiced Poached Pears

ACTIVE TIME
15 MINUTES

TOTAL TIME
40 MINUTES

**Serves
2 to 4**

VEGAN

Poached pears make an elegant dessert that's not very filling. They're perfect for the end of a heavier meal, but don't stop there. They're great for breakfast too; poach them as directed, then cut the poached halves into chunks and serve with their sauce over waffles or oatmeal.

2 large pears

1 cup medium-dry white wine (such as a dry-style Riesling or Gewurztraminer)

½ cup brandy or cognac

⅓ cup brown sugar

1 strip orange peel

5 or 6 whole cloves

1 cinnamon stick, broken into 2 or 3 pieces

2 or 3 cardamom pods (optional)

1. Peel, halve, and core the pears. Leave the stem on or remove.

2. Place the Dutch oven over medium heat. Add the wine, brandy, brown sugar, orange peel, cloves, cinnamon and cardamom (if using). Bring to a simmer, stirring until the sugar dissolves.

3. Add the pears. Turn the heat down to maintain a bare simmer, and cover the pot. Cook for 15 to 20 minutes, or until a knife inserted into one of the pears goes in easily.

4. Use tongs or a slotted spoon to transfer the pears to two bowls.

5. Turn the heat up to medium-high and bring the liquid to a boil. Cook until it's reduced to a thin syrup, about 4 minutes. Remove the orange peel, cloves, cinnamon stick, and cardamom pods. Pour the warm syrup over the pears and serve.

INGREDIENT TIP If you would like leftovers, you can add two more pears to the same amount of poaching liquid. The liquid works equally well with apples, which may take a little more time to become tender.

Crème Caramel

ACTIVE TIME
15 MINUTES

TOTAL TIME
55 MINUTES
PLUS CHILL TIME

**Makes
4 small
custards**

VEGETARIAN

Here's a great shortcut: Instead of making my own caramel, I use a high-quality store-bought caramel sauce. Although slightly richer than the usual caramel (which is just caramelized sugar with no cream or butter added), it works quite well in this recipe and is much less fussy.

¼ cup caramel sauce

1½ cups whole milk

1 teaspoon vanilla extract

½ cup sugar

2 eggs plus 1 egg yolk

1. Preheat the oven to 325°F.

2. Set four empty 1-cup custard cups or ramekins in the Dutch oven and add enough water to come up to within ½ inch of the tops of the ramekins. Remove the ramekins and heat the water over medium-high heat just until simmering. As soon as the water reaches a simmer, turn off the heat and place the pot in the oven.

3. Divide the caramel sauce evenly among the ramekins.

4. While the water heats, add the milk to a 2-cup measuring cup and stir in the vanilla. In the microwave, heat just to a simmer (or you can do this in a saucepan on the stove). While the milk heats, add the eggs and egg yolk and sugar to a small bowl and whisk for about 2 minutes or until the mixture turns slightly pale.

5. Slowly pour in the milk until the mixture is homogeneous; no streaks of egg should remain. Strain the mixture through a small sieve into the ramekins. Pour slowly so as to disturb the caramel as little as possible. Cover each ramekin with a square of aluminum foil.

6. Carefully place the ramekins in the Dutch oven. Bake the custards, uncovered by the Dutch oven lid, for 35 to 40 minutes, or until the custard is set (remove the foil and gently wiggle one to check; the center should not be liquid). Carefully remove the Dutch oven and then, using tongs, remove the ramekins from the water. Let cool for 5 to 10 minutes, then refrigerate for at least 2 hours to set.

7. To serve, you can unmold the custards onto plates, so that the caramel is on top. To do so, run the tip of a knife or small offset spatula around the sides of the custards. Place a small plate with a rim over the ramekin and turn the whole thing upside down. Tap the bottom of the ramekin, and the custard and sauce should release. Or, if you prefer, just eat the custard in the ramekin.

Appendix A
Dutch Oven Care and Maintenance

Dutch ovens are substantial vessels, and they might seem indestructible. For the most part, they are, but even elephants and Abrams tanks can be laid low by seemingly minor maladies. Here are a few cautions to keep in mind, and a few rules to follow.

> Although enamel coatings are durable and easy to clean, they are susceptible to chipping, especially at the rims of pots and lids, exposing the raw iron underneath. If you discover a chip, apply a dab of oil to the naked metal after washing.

> When you store your pot, take care not to jostle it against other cookware. That's how enamel gets chipped.

> Avoid extreme and rapid temperature changes (for instance, going straight from the heat to a sink full of chilly soaking water), especially with enameled pieces (although even plain cast iron can crack if it's subject to wild environmental swings. The coating and the metal it protects expand and contract at different rates.

> Enamel coatings are, if gently coaxed, capable of withstanding pretty high heat. The same is not true of the plastic lid knobs sported by many brands. Either avoid temperatures higher than 375°F, or replace the originals with more resistant metal knobs.

> For baked-on food, soaking is your friend—even for plain cast iron (assuming it's properly seasoned). An hour or two in hot water laced with dishwashing liquid will loosen almost anything.

> If soaking doesn't work, enameled cast iron can be cleaned with a non-abrasive cleaner like Bar Keeper's Friend or Bon Ami. (You can use these products on plain cast iron, too, but they will destroy the seasoning.)

> If you discover rust on your non-enameled Dutch oven, use Bar Keeper's Friend or Bon Ami to remove it. If those don't work, try soaking in Coca-Cola (it's laced with phosphoric acid, the same active ingredient in naval jelly), and using a scouring pad. In any case, you'll have to season your pot again, but you already know how to do that (page 12).

Chances are, your enameled cast iron Dutch oven will never look as pretty as it does the minute it comes out of the box, so take a picture if you want to remember it. However, a lot of stains (usually brownish) will come out by boiling a one-part enzymatic laundry detergent with four parts water solution in the pot for ten minutes. Throw out the solution, then wash and dry as usual.

Appendix B
The Clean Fifteen & the Dirty Dozen

A nonprofit environmental watchdog organization called Environmental Working Group (EWG) looks at data supplied by the U.S. Department of Agriculture (USDA) and the Food and Drug Administration (FDA) about pesticide residues. Each year it compiles a list of the best and worst pesticide loads found in commercial crops. You can use these lists to decide which fruits and vegetables to buy organic to minimize your exposure to pesticides and which produce is considered safe enough to buy conventionally. This does not mean they are pesticide-free, though, so wash these fruits and vegetables thoroughly.

These lists change every year, so make sure you look up the most recent one before you fill your shopping cart. You'll find the most recent lists as well as a guide to pesticides in produce at EWG.org/FoodNews.

2016 Dirty Dozen

Apples
Celery
Cherries
Cherry tomatoes
Cucumbers
Grapes
Nectarines
Peaches
Spinach
Strawberries
Sweet bell peppers
Tomatoes

In addition to the Dirty Dozen, the EWG added two types of produce contaminated with highly toxic organo-phosphate insecticides:

Kale/
collard greens
Hot peppers

2016 Clean Fifteen

Asparagus
Avocados
Cabbage
Cantaloupes
(domestic)
Cauliflower
Eggplants
Grapefruits
Honeydew Melons
Kiwis
Mangos
Onions

Papayas
Pineapples
Sweet corn
Sweet peas
(frozen)

Appendix C

Measurement Conversions

Volume Equivalents (Liquid)

U.S. STANDARD	U.S. STANDARD (OUNCES)	METRIC (APPROXIMATE)
2 tablespoons	1 fl. oz.	30 mL
¼ cup	2 fl. oz.	60 mL
½ cup	4 fl. oz.	120 mL
1 cup	8 fl. oz.	240 mL
1½ cups	12 fl. oz.	355 mL
2 cups or 1 pint	16 fl. oz.	475 mL
4 cups or 1 quart	32 fl. oz.	1 L
1 gallon	128 fl. oz.	4 L

Oven Temperatures

FAHRENHEIT (F)	CELSIUS (C) (APPROXIMATE)
250°	120°
300°	150°
325°	165°
350°	180°
375°	190°
400°	200°
425°	220°
450°	230°

Volume Equivalents (Dry)

U.S. STANDARD	METRIC (APPROXIMATE)
⅛ teaspoon	0.5 mL
¼ teaspoon	1 mL
½ teaspoon	2 mL
¾ teaspoon	4 mL
1 teaspoon	5 mL
1 tablespoon	15 mL
¼ cup	59 mL
⅓ cup	79 mL
½ cup	118 mL
⅔ cup	156 mL
¾ cup	177 mL
1 cup	235 mL
2 cups or 1 pint	475 mL
3 cups	700 mL
4 cups or 1 quart	1 L

Weight Equivalents

U.S. STANDARD	METRIC (APPROXIMATE)
½ ounce	15 g
1 ounce	30 g
2 ounces	60 g
4 ounces	115 g
8 ounces	225 g
12 ounces	340 g
16 ounces or 1 pound	455 g

Index

Acknowledgments

I would like to thank Matt South and his staff at The Cook's Warehouse. Thanks to the great editorial and design team at Rockridge Press, who worked so hard to create a beautiful book. And finally, thanks to Dave, Caitlin, and Eric, who put up with endless recipe testing with very few complaints.

About the Author

Janet A. Zimmerman is the author of *All About Cooking for Two: A Very Quick Guide* and *The Healthy Pressure Cooker Cookbook: Nourishing Meals Made Fast*. For more than 15 years, she has been teaching culinary classes and writing about food for publications and websites such as *Martha Stewart Living* and NPR's Kitchen Window blog. She's twice been published in the anthology *Best Food Writing* and is a recipient of the Bert Greene Journalism Award from the International Association of Culinary Professionals. Janet and her partner Dave live in Atlanta, Georgia.

CPSIA information can be obtained
at www.ICGtesting.com
Printed in the USA
BVOW11s1457061116

466333BV00001B/1/P